Published by **Inspired By Learning**

Copyright © 2014 Inspired By Learning and John

Published in Aberdeen, Scotland.

Printed in Scotland.

How to cite this book:

Darwin, J (2014) Mindfulness Based Life Enhancement. Aberdeen: Inspired By Learning.

Find us on the web at www.inspiredbylearning.eu

Web Design by Mario Jagar, Zagreb, Croatia

Cover and Text Design, Graphics and Formatting by Ita Dukić, Zadar, Croatia

ISBN: 978-1-909876-04-0 (paperback)

978-1-909876-05-7 (e-book)

Reflecting the author's commitment to gender equality, gender specific terms, such as 'he' and 'she' are used intermittently throughout this book.

Every effort has been made by Inspired By Learning to obtain the necessary permissions with reference to copyright material, both illustrative and textual. We apologize for any omissions in this respect and will be pleased to make the appropriate acknowledgements and references in any future edition.

Figure 7.1 'Knowledge Conversion' on page 149 is from The Knowledge Creating Company by Nonaka and Takeuchi (1995) Figs. 3-3, 3-4 pp.71-72, and is used by permission of Oxford University Press, USA.

Contact: info@inspiredbylearning.eu

GRATITUDE

I am grateful to many people for their help and support in my journey of mindful discovery. So I would like to express my gratitude to:

- My meditation and Buddhism teachers, in particular Rev Peter, Rev Leandra and Michael Chaskalson
- My yoga and Qigong teachers – Eric, Gary, Graham, Nidhi, Pat, Polly, Leslie, Wendy – I have learnt much from you all!
- My teachers at the University of Aberdeen and the Mindfulness Association, and in particular David McMurtry for first suggesting this book and supporting it all the way to publication
- My fellow students when I was taking the MSc in Mindfulness Studies
- My colleagues at SHU, including Ann Macaskill, Beverley Macmillan, Ian Maher, Sue Marriott, Alec Melling, Barbara Reid and Mike Pupius
- The many participants in the MBLE courses who provided feedback and helped me improve the programme, and in particular the 100+ who are members of the Continuation Community
- The many fine writers who have given me inspiration in developing MBLE
- And most of all, Denise for her support and love.

John Darwin,

May 2014.

"Mindfulness-based life enhancement is a beautifully written, well-informed and inspiring exploration into how practising mindfulness can indeed enhance our lives. Linked to an eight week mindfulness training course, it offers insights into both Buddhist and secular writings on mindfulness along with philosophical and positive psychological ones. It tackles the thorny issue of the relationship between mindfulness and compassion training and highlights the importance of the link between attention and intention (motivation) - it is the intention that sets the course and how our minds become organised. Diagrams and summaries are immensely useful. A book to treasure and come back to repeatedly."

Professor Paul Gilbert OBE

"John Darwin's book is important because it brings mindfulness into perspective as a mind training for everybody - not just in a clinical or monastic setting. Over recent years there has been a lot written about positive thinking, and much of this has generated unrealistic expectations in people's minds, giving rise to ideas of 'getting rid' of painful emotions and painting them over with preferred, nice feelings. This often leads to suppression, self deception and disappointment. John avoids this, and instead offers a well reasoned option based on his understanding of positive psychology and Buddhist training in ethics and loving-kindness. He offers practical methods for challenging tendencies towards negative thinking about ourselves and others, and goes on to teach how we can instead enhance our positive potential in a practical way in our daily living situations.

His presentation is well reasoned and includes directions to people who plan to become mindfulness teachers. He also offers a wealth of useful diagrams and tables depicting the stages of training and how these bring about changes in the mind. If you want both a practical guide to becoming mindful and an exposition of how the process works, this is the book you have been looking for."

Rob Nairn, International Mindfulness Teacher and Author

"A valuable contribution to mindfulness literature that highlights the importance of focusing on positive emotions and cultivating our innate capacity for compassion. Indeed, if we do not do so we run the risk of mindfulness practice being undermined by darker motivational forces. John Darwin skilfully integrates the four immeasurable qualities of love, compassion, joy and equanmimity into his Mindfulness Based Life Enhancement programme. For anyone practising at the cutting edge of mindfulness and compassion, this book is highly recommended."

Choden, Mindfulness and Compassion Teacher and Author

"This book charts a journey in Mindfulness Based Life Enhancement. Drawing on a range of disciplines, it introduces a number of themes to both challenge and inspire those who wish to explore the benefits of living a more mindful life. It offers an opportunity to learn and reflect on both philosophy and practice; the first-person accounts are refreshing in their honesty and provide insight into how mindfulness practice has supported people in finding equanimity and developing resilience. It is undoubtedly a book to savour."

Sue Marriott, Deputy Head, Department of Management, Sheffield Business School

Contents

1. Introduction

This book draws on a four year exploration of mindfulness. Retirement is often seen in our ageist society as an end-point - the conclusion to a productive life. I chose instead, like many of my friends, to see it as a time for new adventure, including this exploration which has unexpectedly turned into a fourth 'career'. After forty years as first a community activist, then a local government officer, and finally an academic, I now find myself teaching a subject which at first sight might seem far removed from those. But I hope to demonstrate here that there are exciting links to be made - and that mindfulness is very relevant in all settings.

Central to this book is Mindfulness Based Life Enhancement (MBLE), an approach to mindfulness which forms the basis for a course taught in Sheffield and elsewhere. Like many Mindfulness Based Interventions (MBIs) this is an eight-week course, including a Day of Practice and regular home activity [there is also a six week version]. Unlike some MBIs it is non-clinical and open to everyone. The core philosophy is that mindfulness is as much about increasing the positive as it is about reducing the negative; hence the name Life Enhancement.

The course was not originally part of my adventure, which I saw as a personal project to deepen my existing practice (Zazen), exploring the theory of mindfulness and Buddhism in greater detail, recognising the need for "equal emphasis on all three aspects of the Buddhist discipline - moral conduct, concentration and wisdom" (Ch'en 1964:399). Besides re-engaging with the work of Kabat-Zinn (1990), which I had first read some years earlier, and more generally Mindfulness Based Interventions, I read the Nikaya (Nanamoli and Bodhi 2005; Nyanaponika Thera and Bodhi 2007; Walshe 1995), and for the first time seriously explored the Four Immeasurables (that I only did this forty years after my initial exploration of Zen demonstrates the narrowness of my previous stance).

---

[1] The Nikaya are the early Buddhist texts, which were brought together in five collections.

But links with my interests in teaching and organisational theory repeatedly emerged, and when University colleagues expressed an interest in mindfulness I gave two staff lectures, on mindfulness, organisations and higher education. The interest level far exceeded expectations, and several people asked if I would be running an eight-week course. An email to people attending the two lectures, inviting expressions of interest in a course, brought more than 15 applicants[2].

The course to be developed would:

- not be offered as therapy, but rather as a course suitable for all
- be based on mindfulness, incorporating this explicitly, but extended in various ways
- include a positive focus
- explicitly introduce the Four Immeasurables
- incorporate purpose.

As this first course was oversubscribed there was clearly greater demand. Further, the time involved in preparing the format, content, guidebooks and CDs made it worthwhile to offer further courses. This led me to consider evaluation, both for my own benefit, so that I could improve the programme, and also to find out whether it actually made a difference to participants. As I have been involved in research projects (often action research) throughout my three careers, I decided to approach this in the same spirit, by designing a wider action research project, incorporating evaluation and feedback methods into it.

It is a cliché (much loved by academics!) that the best way to learn is to teach. Two decades of University teaching have convinced me that this has substance, and the experience of teaching MBLE has proved immensely valuable. The initial decision to run a course meant that I needed to reflect on the mindfulness courses in which I had participated, think through structure, content and process, consider the role of the facilitator, and how it related to my existing experience as a teacher. Alongside the deep learning that has come

---

[2] This is the maximum I like to take, both in terms of group size and room space.

from running the course ten times, with over 140 participants, I have also continued to study, in particular by taking and completing the Master's Degree in Mindfulness offered by the University of Aberdeen. And in line with the Zen aphorism that one should never confuse the finger pointing at the moon with the moon itself I have continued, and indeed enhanced, my personal practice.

This book is not a guide to mindfulness: there are already many excellent works that do this, some of which are referenced later, and it would be redundant to add to this rapidly growing body of literature. The intention rather is to review a particular way of approaching and practising mindfulness for people who wish to take advantage of the many benefits to be gained from a more mindful life.

MBLE draws upon Buddhist philosophy and psychology, as well as a variety of other disciplines, including Ancient Greek philosophy, social psychology, positive psychology, and learning theory. One of my concerns was that the Buddhist background should not be an impediment to those with different (or no) religious convictions. As we shall see later, this has not been a problem - indeed for many the fact that the course has strong foundations is seen as a distinct advantage. Martine Batchelor has commented (2011:159-60) in relation to MBCT that it is in accordance with the four great efforts as taught by the Buddha, which she renders as follows:

1. To cultivate conditions so that negative states that have not arisen do not arise
2. To let go of negative states once they have arisen
3. To cultivate the conditions that enable positive states to arise
4. To sustain positive states once they have arisen.

MBLE accords with these also, and there is as much emphasis on the third and fourth as there is on the first two.

The first part of this book explains Mindfulness Based Life Enhancement. In Chapters Two to Four I explore the four key components of Mindfulness Based Life Enhancement: mindfulness, mindful learning, the Four Immeasurables, and Positive Psychology. Throughout I draw on comments from MBLE participants to illustrate key themes. In Chapter Five I bring these together, showing the structure and content of the course, comparing this to several other programmes developed in recent years. I also describe the process involved – Action Learning.

In the second part of the book I first evaluate the course, drawing on a variety of methods, and drawing in particular on the first-person experience of myself and the participants. I then extend the discussion to reflect on what has been learnt, and give a specific example by considering the implications for senior citizens. Even if you are not one, this should be of interest to you, because you hopefully will be in the fullness of time! My argument is that Mindfulness Based Life Enhancement has much to offer. In Chapter Nine I extend this argument to show what mindfulness based enhanced living involves.

2. MINDFULNESS, LEARNING AND CHANGE

> In this Chapter we look at mindfulness, and four themes which help its enhancement - the two darts, the automatic pilot, the relationship between formal and informal mindfulness, and the Beginner's Mind. We relate Beginner's Mind to mindful learning, and from this develop the concept of Mindful Competence.

MINDFULNESS

The approach to mindfulness adopted in Mindfulness Based Life Enhancement is that found in most courses: it is "Knowing what is happening, while it is happening, without preference" (Nairn 1999:27). Kabat-Zinn's (1990:33-40) well-known characterisation comprises seven aspects:

- Non-judging: Impartial witnessing, observing the present, moment by moment without evaluation and categorization
- Non-striving: Non-goal-oriented, remaining unattached to outcome or achievement, not forcing things
- Acceptance: Open to seeing and acknowledging things as they are in the present moment, acceptance does not mean passivity or resignation, rather a clearer understanding of the present so one can more effectively respond
- Patience: Allowing things to unfold in their time, bringing patience to ourselves, to others, and to the present moment
- Trust: Trusting oneself, one's body, intuition, emotions as well as trusting that life is unfolding as it is supposed to
- Openness (Beginner's Mind): Seeing things as if for the first time, creating possibility by paying attention to all feedback in the present moment
- Letting go: Nonattachment, not holding on to thoughts, feelings, experiences; however, letting go does not mean suppressing.

Shapiro and Schwartz (2000) subsequently added five more – gentleness, generosity, empathy, gratitude and loving-kindness. These will feature in the discussion in the next two chapters.

When introducing mindfulness to people new to the idea, four themes have proved particularly helpful. One is the Beginner's Mind: this is so important that it deserves a fuller discussion. Before that, it is worth briefly considering the other three themes which help people develop a greater appreciation of mindfulness.

THE TWO DARTS

In the Sallatha Sutta the Buddha explains that pain can be disentangled from suffering. Using the metaphor of two darts, he describes the first dart as unavoidable – perhaps a painful feeling or longer term sickness, a painful comment from someone else. So this can be either physical or mental pain. But the second dart we fire ourselves, and this causes mental suffering which compounds the issue. This may be in the form of rumination – thinking about how unpleasant the pain is, feeling sorry for ourselves because we are ill, or resenting the way we were spoken to by someone, and dwelling upon how unpleasant they have been. The practice of mindfulness cannot prevent the first dart, but it can address the second: *"It is as if a man were pierced by a dart, but was not hit by a second dart following the first one. So this person experiences feelings caused by a single dart only."* The Mindful Space provides the moment of choice, where it becomes possible to reject the automatic pilot and instead choose a different course (see Exhibit 1).

Frankl argues that even in the most extreme circumstances of concentration camps it is possible for a human to retain *"the last of the human freedoms – to choose one's attitude in any given set of circumstances … Every human being has the freedom to change at any instant"* (2004:53, 105). The Two Darts proves a powerful metaphor for people to keep in their mind, noticing the many times they are about to fire the second dart, and developing the ability to choose not to do this.

- I try to be more alert. It doesn't always happen. I can go for hours without pulling myself up short and thinking 'be here now', but when I do, I find it very valuable. I'm more aware, therefore, of autopilot, of negativity bias, of the second dart.
- A bit calmer, more grounded, less firing that second dart. Not perfect yet though!
- Am able to have some perspective and I use particular things such as the Dart to prevent me ruminating or getting into a worry cycle.
- It's only recently that I've made a definite effort to get up half an hour earlier in order to do some meditation and yoga. It helps to make me more aware of how my body is feeling; the potentially harmful effects of rehearse/rehashing; the two darts effect, etc. Basically, going on a mindfulness course has the potential to help you really live in the moment - something so many of us truly struggle with.

THE AUTOMATIC PILOT - RECOGNISING ITS NATURE AND IMPACT

Closely linked to the Two Darts is the Automatic Pilot. We do many things without thinking about them, and often this is very valuable. But it can also take the form of automatic, and unhelpful, triggers to inappropriate action – for example firing the second dart. In Exhibit 2 we see examples of people's growing recognition of this.

Exhibit 2: COMMENTS OF PARTICIPANTS IN MBLE COURSE: AUTOMATIC PILOT

- One of the reasons for doing the mindfulness course was to manage the change in my life of redundancy. I do feel different having done the course and people have remarked how calm and positive I seem. I have surprised myself and found hidden depths of resilience which has given me confidence. I am noticing the habits of automatic pilot and the triggers and noticing how I choose to respond to them, rightly or wrongly.
- I found this course really helpful. Before I came along I was feeling burnt out, low in energy, constantly worrying about 'to do lists' and anxious. I had no idea of the impact these 'automatic pilot' thought patterns were having on me from a physiological point of view. Even when I found time to relax, I was still lacking the skills in being able to switch off and as a result my batteries had almost spent. I had been wanting to learn more about mindfulness for over a year, so it was ideal when the opportunity arose to attend the course.
- It has helped me with stress reduction, it has helped me be mindful in carrying out activities and getting me out of automatic pilot.
- Am much less likely to go onto automatic pilot now. I do gentle yoga movements most days. Although I had done a yoga class for a year, I never did it at home before because I couldn't remember any movements and I also felt I had to learn some complicated sequence. Whereas I learnt from you that just a bit of gentle mindful movement and yoga a day is fine! I find the breathing and movement very calming.

THE RELATIONSHIP BETWEEN FORMAL AND INFORMAL MINDFULNESS

Formal practice involves a variety of mindfulness meditations (sitting, lying down, walking, gentle yoga). Informal practice is about having mindful moments throughout the day where you are conscious of what you are doing and experiencing, and comments from several MBLE participants give specific examples of informal mindfulness practice (see Exhibit 3). A key principle in MBLE is that the former helps to enrich the latter.

Exhibit 3: COMMENTS OF PARTICIPANTS: INFORMAL MINDFULNESS

- Mindful eating; awareness of nature/senses (sounds, sights, body sensations); mindful exercise – for example running and breathing.
- Phone app prompting to 'consider' various things. Three minute breathing space; walking, swimming; general awareness of trying to live more in the present moment.
- Whilst swimming, sitting in traffic jams, at work, stopping and giving myself some breathing space at work.
- Tuning into breathing during other activities throughout the day.
- Yes - short "being here now" episodes when I remember to.
- I've started setting my mobile phone alarm to remind me to stop, breathe, relax. I also try to remember to really talk to people rather than go on auto-pilot conversations, to do random acts of kindness, to do mindful check-ins.
- Mindful eating - try to do this for one meal a day; mindful shower - everyday mindful walking - not as slowly as we do when we meet but slowly any number of tasks around the house - when I remember. Whilst decorating recently, I practiced mindfulness and found the job a lot easier.

- I used to meditate daily and may well come back to it at some point. However, I try to integrate a practice of mindfulness into as many activities as possible in my everyday life. It is relatively straightforward with the more mundane, repetitive activities, such as washing up and walking to work. Mindfulness in relating to others is particularly important but much more difficult. Trying to concentrate solely on one activity e.g. cycling mindfully.
- Much more able to carry out informal mindfulness, and do it often. So my runs in the park are much more enjoyable and I find myself stopping and looking at the twinkling river or the sky/clouds/leaves, and listening. Now at the end of my run I sit on a bench and do some breathing whilst listening to sounds, feeling the rain/wind/sun on my face. It makes me smile a lot more when I am running in the park now. I'm less likely now to worry and ruminate about things as I run.

Underpinning all of these is the relationship between mindfulness and change, which relates also to the case made for mindfulness. Thus, if we consider the various findings summarised in Table 2.1, we can see that the common factor is change. People join mindfulness courses because they want to achieve change: they see mindfulness as a faculty which can be developed: "a steady work of cultivating and developing something which is latent" (Nairn 1999:22).

Table 2.1: THE CASE FOR MINDFULNESS
Improves aspects of attention (Jha, Krompinger, Baime 2007; Lutz et al 2008).
Increases immune functioning and produces brain changes consistent with more effective handling of emotions under stress (Davidson et al 2003).
Reduces negative mood, perceived stress and rumination (Ortner, Kilner, Zelazo 2007).
Reduces anxiety levels (Halliwell 2010).

Increases control of behaviour (Halliwell 2010).
Reduces symptoms of burnout and improves life satisfaction among health professionals (Mackenzie, Poulin, Seidman-Carlson 2006).
May improve ability to maintain preparedness and orient attention (Shapiro et al 2007).
May improve ability to process information quickly and accurately (Shapiro et al 2007).
Can support the development of creativity (Shapiro et al 2007).
Supports and enhances the development of skills needed for interpersonal relationships (Shapiro et al 2007).
Increases empathetic responses (Shapiro et al 2007).
Helps resist unwanted situational influences (Zimbardo 2007).

Yet mindfulness courses emphasise acceptance, and being-mode rather than doing-mode. The advice is to accept all that is happening and *"recognize all this without trying to manage our experience in any way, without pulling away"* (Brach 2003:27). Nairn comments *"Change will come about if we learn to work skilfully with the mind but we don't make change the goal"* (1999:9).

Linehan argues that *"The paradox of change versus acceptance runs throughout therapy"* (1993:208), while Rogers sees the paradox in a way that supports Nairn's comment: *"The curious paradox is that when I accept myself just as I am, then I change. We cannot change, we cannot move away from what we are, until we thoroughly accept what we are. Then change seems to come about almost unnoticed." (1961:17).* Or as Brach puts it *"I have discovered again and again that bringing Radical Acceptance to any part of our experience is the fundamental shift that opens the way to genuine, lasting change"* (2003:38).

As we have seen, for Kabat-Zinn acceptance involves *"a clearer understanding of the present so one can more effectively respond"* (1990), and this can be developed by considering the relationship between **means** and **ends**. People come to mindfulness with objectives and intentions, which may well include the changes identified in Table 2.1, or more generally enhancement of their daily living. *"Your intentions set the stage for what is possible. They remind you from moment to moment of why you are practising in the first place … I used to think that meditation practice was so powerful . . . that as long as you did it at all, you would see growth and change. But time has taught me that some kind of personal vision is also necessary"* (1990:32,46). For Shapiro et al (2006) intention is one of the three axioms of mindfulness, along with attention and attitude.

Initially therefore people may well see mindfulness as the **means** to these **ends**. But when involved in the various practices taught on the course, it is essential that they 'bracket' these Ends and focus on the practice itself, which thereby become the End. And the same can apply to informal mindfulness. An illustration which often helps people to see this is Thich Nhat Hanh's well-known example (1991:4) of dish washing. My **intention** when washing dishes is to get them clean, but while actually doing it my **attention** becomes my **intention** - I wash the dishes to wash the dishes. Similarly one may practise yoga with the intention of maintaining fitness and flexibility, but during the actual practice detailed **attention** to each movement becomes the **intention** (see Box 1).

So the intention in practising meditation is developing the faculty of mindfulness, but while actually meditating the **attention** becomes the **intention** - bare awareness, and thus direct experience. This is expressed in Dogen's Rules for Meditation, where he advises us to *"sit steadily, neither trying to think nor trying not to think; just sitting, with no deliberate thought is the important aspect of serene reflection meditation"* (Dogen in Jiyu-Kennett 1993:98). Suzuki's lectures enrich this, in particular the emphasis on breathing:

"When we practice Zazen our mind always follows our breathing. When we inhale, the air comes into the inner world. When we exhale, the air goes out to the outer world. … So when we practice Zazen, all that exists is the movement of the breathing, but we are aware of this movement. …. When you practice Zazen, just practice Zazen. If enlightenment comes, it just comes. We should not attach to the attainment" (1970:29, 60).

This distinction between ends and means is recognised also in MBCT: "*As central as the formal mindfulness practices were in MBCT, we did not see them as an endpoint, but rather as the training ground for the types of skills in attention deployment, curiosity, kindness and grounding that would help participants respond to real challenges in their everyday lives*" (Segal et al 2013:383). In relation to the Three Minute Breathing Space they comment: "As with all meditation practices, if we become too goal-oriented about it, we'll revert from being mode back into doing mode, thereby reducing our chances for new learning" (ibid:385).

Box 1: MINDFUL MOVEMENT

Clarifying the relationship between means and ends also applies to mindful movement, and here I draw on personal experience relating to one of my regular practices, Pilates. This is frequently promoted as a good way to lose weight and look better[3] , and it is easy to fall into this mindset, where the end becomes dominant. Listening more carefully to my Pilates teachers, I realised that they expressed, explicitly or implicitly, underlying principles and it has proved valuable to explore these in the literature.

Joseph Pilates[4] himself identified six principles: concentration, centring, control, breath, precision and flow principles which fit well with the notion of 'mindful movement' (Muscolino & Cipriani 2004).

My overall Intention now with Pilates remains that of fitness and of gradual improvement in my agility and capability, but while actually doing a class, the Intention becomes mindful movement. I quickly found that foregrounding these principles enhanced my practice, and the same has applied to yoga, tai chi and QiGong. In each class what becomes important is to 'bracket' wider objectives, and focus closely on the movement itself.

---

[3] For example "get slim and sexy" (http://www.malibupilates.co.uk/about_malibu_pilates.aspx); "work your body into the long, lean sexy look you've always had" (http://www.winsorpilates.com/)
[4] Muscolino & Cipriani, (2004)

This relationship between Ends and Means is summarised in Table 2.2. A slight variant of the Three-Minute Breathing Space can be helpful here, with the initial stage being to pause in what one is doing and think "everything I have ever done and been has brought me to this moment, here and now" – a reminder of the sheer value and importance of the present moment.

Table 2.2: ENDS AND MEANS

			Purpose: the aim of the practice: cultivating attention	Action / Change	Developing the faculty of mindfulness	Intention	How it could/ should be
END	Doing	Change					
MEANS	Being	Acceptance	Method: what you do: return to what is already there and rest	Mindfulness	Direct Experience; Bare Awareness	Attention	How it is

Sources: column 2: Segal et al (2002); column 3: Linehan (1993); column 4: McLeod (2001)

Exhibit 4: COMMENTS OF PARTICIPANTS: EXPERIENCE OF THE COURSE

- This course benefited me immensely, in that I have learnt the value in being present to the world around me and that I can overcome the hindrances of ruminations to actually live.
- It gave me hope that I could take control and manage my work-life balance more effectively. It was an oasis in all the chaos!
- The course is a much needed breathing space from work. I wondered if I could spare two hours a week, but in fact it has helped me to be calmer and more productive at work.
- I really enjoyed; it was both calming as well as 'disciplined'- this combination works for me.
- I can't recommend it too highly and cannot imagine that anyone could not benefit from it.
- This is a fantastic opportunity to experience practices that can help transform your life.

MINDFUL LEARNING AND THE BEGINNER'S MIND

Like many interested in mindfulness, I have long been intrigued by Suzuki's idea of the 'beginner's mind': *"this does not mean a closed mind, but actually an empty mind and a ready mind. If your mind is empty, it is always ready for anything; it is open to everything"* (1970:21). The contrast frequently made is between this and the expert mind, with the exhortation *"always to keep your beginner's mind"* (ibid:22). But in the spirit of Zen, this is not either/or. The expert mind has its value: for example, Pasteur argued that *"in the fields of observation chance favours only the prepared mind"*[5] and it is unwise to discount this. As Richmond, an ordained disciple of Suzuki, puts it *"This is the paradox of humility, and of the Learner's Work. To learn as adults - to truly learn - we must simultaneously be of a mind like a young child and be fully cognizant of all that we already know"* (2004:194).

To resolve this apparent paradox, I have adapted the 'conscious competence learning model'[6] (Figure 2-1). Conventionally the model has four stages. In Stage 1 - Unconscious Incompetence - you are not aware of the existence or relevance of the skill area, or that you have a particular deficiency in the area concerned. You need to become conscious of your incompetence before development of the new skill or learning can begin. In Stage 2 - Conscious Incompetence - you become aware of the existence and relevance of the skill, and also of your deficiency in this area. You recognise that by improving your skill or ability in this area your effectiveness will improve.

In Stage 3 you achieve 'conscious competence' in a skill when you can perform it reliably at will, but will need to concentrate and think in order to perform the skill, which is not yet automatic. Further practice leads to Stage 4 - Unconscious Competence - where the skill enters the unconscious parts of your brain; it becomes 'second nature'. This is often characterised as performing with 'automatic pilot', enabling you to do other things at the same time (for example, talking while driving, listening to the radio while typing).

---

[5] Retrieved from http://en.wikiquote.org/wiki/Louis_Pasteur. Originally quoted in Eves (1988).

[6] It is argued at http://www.businessballs.com/consciouscompetencelearningmodel.htm that "the earliest origins of the conscious competence theory are not entirely clear".

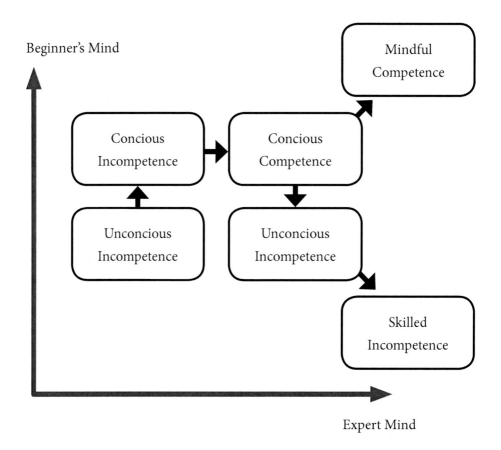

Beginner's Mind

Mindful
Competence

Concious
Incompetence

Concious
Competence

Unconcious
Incompetence

Unconcious
Incompetence

Skilled
Incompetence

Expert Mind

Figure 2-1: THE MINDFUL COMPETENCE MODEL

Throughout daily life there are many tasks which require Unconscious Competence - in addition to driving or typing, we could add walking, computer skills and many other body-mind links. But there is the danger here of falling into Skilled Incompetence, a term introduced by Argyris (1986): "*Skilled incompetence is a condition in which people are very good at doing things that have unhappy consequences, even though they seem like the right thing to do*". In the mindfulness literature there is often reference to the danger of 'automatic pilot' "*functioning mechanically, without being fully aware of what we are doing or experiencing*" (Kabat-Zinn, 1990:21). This is sometimes characterised as mindlessness: "*A style of mental functioning in which people follow recipes, impose old categories to classify what they see, act with some rigidity, operate on automatic pilot, and mislabel unfamiliar new contexts as familiar old ones. A mindless mental style works to conceal problems that are worsening"* (Weick and Sutcliffe, 2007:88).

Sliding into Skilled Incompetence is the dangerous possibility which arises once the practitioner has reached the stage of Unconscious Competence. Segal et al (2002:72ff) identify the way in which our skill in conceptual problem solving can translate into (incompetent) rumination. Similarly, with driving it is argued that *"the major cause, which contributes to about 95% of all road accidents, is human error"*, and that consequently *"you should be in the correct frame of mind for driving … concentrate and stay alive"*(Stacey 1995:11ff). Concerns have also been expressed in the field of medicine. Moulton et al (2007:S111) report that Bereiter and Scardamalia have suggested that burnout, disillusionment, and complacency can lead to experts acting in less thoughtful, non-reflective ways. As a result, doctors might begin to "process" patients, rather than engaging in thoughtful reflection of the complexities of clinical cases.

Recognition of these concerns leads to three extensions of the original diagram. **First**, we add Skilled Incompetence. **Second**, we add two axes: the vertical axis relates to the extent to which the person is employing 'Beginner's Mind'; the horizontal axis relates to the use of 'Expert Mind'. Garrett et al (2009), reviewing analyses of expertise since the mid-1980s, identify a number of ways in which experts have the advantage on others. They solve problems differently, process more quickly, and can access knowledge better. Berliner (2001) contrasts the expert with the novice. Experts recognize meaningful patterns faster, and expert knowledge is structured better for use in performances. Experts also develop automaticity in their behaviour to allow conscious processing of more complex information, and are usually more constrained by task requirements and the social constraints of a situation than are novices. Both make a strong case for maintaining the Expert Mind, while recognising that automaticity is a component in the expert's repertoire.

Thus the objective is not one of moving to unconscious competence, with the dangers of slipping into skilled incompetence, but rather maintaining both the

Beginner's Mind *"ready for anything, open to everything"* (Suzuki op.cit. p21) and the Expert Mind. Levinthal and Rerup (2006) develop a similar argument when they challenge the tendency to "stereotype the two processes" of mindful and less-mindful behaviour, and thereby neglect the interrelationships between them. The former requires the ability effectively to carry out novel action in a flexible manner, coupled with a sustained high level of attention. The latter involves routine-driven behaviour and reinforcement learning - the development and operation of automatic pilot.

The objective therefore is to achieve 'Conscious Competence' in a skill, but then maintain mindfulness while performing it. This we characterise as Mindful Competence, which is the **third** addition to the original diagram. I first came across a version of this approach in Richmond's idea of 'control by paying attention', being actively engaged as a participant noticing what is really happening and waiting for the right moment to act (1999). I have frequently used this in my work, especially when facilitating Whole Systems Events (which have involved up to 250 people working together in the same room). To do this successfully it is essential that Attention becomes the Intention, paying close attention to everything happening in the room (which may involve 20 tables with animated conversations taking place at each), and being ready to intervene appropriately, help synthesise outcomes, and move the event forward to a successful action-oriented conclusion. Thus my expertise in facilitation (such as it is!) is important, but by paying attention I avoid the danger of the expert mind seeing only a few possibilities.

Langer gives an example of the value of integrating beginner's mind and expert mind: "I have wondered what might happen if hospitals teamed up novices and experts. They do that now of course, but the novices are supposed to learn from the experts and not the other way around. In my scheme, the learning would be mutual. They would be taught to respect that an expert may see what only her training can show her and the novice might notice what the expert was trained to miss" (2009:144).

The Automatic Pilot is very valuable, but we need the ability to choose whether it is appropriate in each setting. In effect, we need a 'Mindful Automatic Pilot' to recognise that a particular Automatic Pilot is about to kick in. Williams and Penman (2011:233) talk of 'mindfulness bells' - reminders to stop and attend. Sometimes the Mindful Automatic Pilot can be used to 're-programme' an Automatic Pilot, as Box 2 illustrates.

Box 2: MINDFUL CYCLING

Cycling provides a good illustration of the value of Mindful Competence. My regular journeys require me to use a busy main road with many side roads leading into it, and I am frequently cut up by motorists. Assertiveness is essential to survival in these circumstances, but I realised some time ago that this had moved into dangerous territory - the behaviour of some motorists kicked in an Automatic Pilot of rage which I displayed (for example by hitting the roof of their car), and I was reaching my destination in a state of anger which I could feel throughout my body. My Unconscious Competence in cycling had turned into Skilled Incompetence in terms of my well-being. By shifting to Mindful Competence I have substantially reduced my anger levels, recognising the old Automatic Pilot and now behaving in a much less problematic way [though I still get annoyed!]. More generally, I would argue that cycling in heavy traffic requires expertise which involves elements of automatic processing (keeping an eye on the road for potholes and moving to avoid them) but also needs the beginner's mind, ready for anything (cars coming out of side roads, car doors flung open, pedestrians crossing the road without checking for traffic ... the list is remarkably long!). The same applies to car drivers who follow the advice of the Advanced Motorist's Handbook.

Thus in Mindful Competence:

- The person has achieved 'conscious competence' in a skill, and chooses to concentrate and think in order to perform the skill
- The person could reliably perform the skill without thinking about it, but chooses not to do so
- The person is able to demonstrate the skill to another, and may be able to teach it well to another person
- The person keeps a Beginner's Mind, attending to what is happening and maintaining mindfulness
- The mind is always ready for anything; it is open to everything.

The basic model therefore has three aspects: Acceptance - Temporal Space – Change. It draws inspiration from the Two Darts: one of the main reasons we fire the second dart is that we fall into Automatic Pilot - we do it without thinking. The Temporal Space can give us the opportunity to recognise this, and ultimately choose not to fire the second dart, thus avoiding Automatic Pilot, which is crucial. On occasions I have used this mnemonic to help:

A   Attend and Accept

B   Breathe, Breathe

C   Consider, Choose and Change.

This freedom to choose has been identified also in Western literature, perhaps most notably in Frankl's analysis of survival in Nazi concentration camps: *"We who lived in concentration camps can remember the men who walked through the huts comforting others, giving away their last piece of bread. They may have been few in number, but they offer sufficient proof that everything can be taken from a man but one thing: the last of the human freedoms, to choose one's attitude in any given set of circumstances, to choose one's own way."* (1962:65)

Acceptance, and understanding of what is, creates the temporal space within which the mindful practitioner has this freedom, and thus the ability to make mindful choice. Moulton et al (2007) identify this as the requirement on occasion to slow down: *"Thus, the expert should be able not only to engage a set of effective automatic resources but, also, to use the resulting freed-up cognitive resources to maintain an attentional vigil on the environment, determine whether the automatic resources are functioning effectively in the particular circumstance, and slow down, engaging more effortful processes, when the situation requires it."* It has also been described as the need to *"prevent premature agreement"* (Darwin 2004:1). It allows us to exercise our discriminating wisdom, which *"recognizes when things are harmful or unjust, but also recognizes the causes and conditions that lead to situations of harm or injustice in the first place"* (Neff 2011:74).

Understanding of each aspect is enriched by adding to Kabat-Zinn's characterisation of mindfulness three further contributions. First there are Langer's (1997) three characteristics of mindful learning (Table 2.3). The idea of mindfulness has been used for some years in what Varela et al call "a non-Buddhist and non-meditative sense" (1993:262, referring specifically to the work of Langer (1997)). While some, including Langer, have expressed caution about the relationship between these two discussions of mindfulness, a parallel can be drawn between the potential integration of Mindful Learning into Mindfulness Based Interventions and the integration of CBT into MBCT, as discussed below. So we here support the approach of Boyatzis and McKee (2005) who also bring together the approaches of Langer and Kabat-Zinn, seeing the cognitive openness advocated by the former, and the moment-to-moment awareness of the latter, as both helping to relate mindfulness to leadership.

Table 2.3: MINDFUL LEARNING	
Creation of new categories	"When we make new categories in a mindful way, we pay attention to the situation and the context. Old categories break down and the individual is no longer trapped by stereotypes." (75)
Openness to new information	"The receiving of new information is a basic function of living creatures. Mindfully engaged individuals will actively attend to changed signals." (140)
Awareness of more than one perspective)	"Once we become mindfully aware of views other than our own, we start to realize that there are as many different views as there are different observers. Such awareness is potentially liberating." (79)
Langer 1997	

Second, we can draw upon a much earlier Western tradition, that of the Greek sceptics, and in particular the Pyrrhonist school who advocated three philosophical guidelines (Suber 1996):

- Akatalepsia: Suspicion of Appearances
- Isosthenia: Balancing of Opposite Views
- Epoche: Suspension of Opinion.

As Suber comments: "The Greek word epoche means to check, cease, suspend, stop, or pause in some activity that otherwise or normally occurs" a characterisation very much in keeping with the stress in mindfulness teaching on recognising the role of the automatic pilot.

Third, from the Buddhist tradition, Richmond (1999), a Zen monk turned management consultant, identified a number of themes which, as explained earlier, have proved very helpful in guiding organisational development practice (Table 2.4).

Table 2.4: CONTROLLING BY PAYING ATTENTION	
"Controlling by Paying Attention is something of a paradox. It actually means giving up control, allowing things to happen, letting the unpredictability of the situation surface and play itself out, while we remain actively engaged in the drama, not just as a spectator but as a participant." (189)	
Notice what is really happening	"as opposed to what we imagine is happening. Being attentive to what is not evident to your eyes and ears, being open to what has not yet been said, being aware of the edges of a situation." (192)
Soft gaze	"Attention works best when our focus is rather soft, like the quality of light at dusk. It is the only way to see the whole picture. At the same time, just because this kind of attention is 'soft' does not mean it is passive or disengaged. On the contrary, it is energized and focused." (192-3)
Awareness of the possibility of what things might be	"In twilight, we cannot see the sharp edges of things so clearly, but the possibility of what things might be, including what we ourselves can contribute to the situation, is stronger." (192)
Collaborative communication	"The collaborative style is more interested in drawing the other person out, in listening attentively." (196)
Waiting for the right moment)	"Pay close attention to the situation without saying anything until the right moment. The attention itself becomes a force for change, as well as a way to catch the best moment to intervene." (197)
Richmond 1999	

MINDFUL COMPETENCE

Returning now to the concept of Mindful Competence, we have the three aspects: Mindful Acceptance, Mindful Space, and Mindful Change. Integrating the approaches summarised above, Mindful Acceptance may be characterised as shown in Table 2.5[7]. There is an important addition here, not covered by the five sources cited above. This concerns the relationship of mind to body. "Embody the experience" involves the recognition that we have 'embodied minds' (Varela et al 1993). We are echoing here Joyce's comment "Mr Duffy lived a short distance from his body" (1914), which applies strongly to the Western mindset. All mindfulness programmes stress the importance of mindful movement, and like others MBLE is underpinned by the Four Foundations of Mindfulness (Figure 2-2).

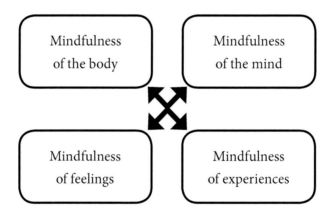

Figure 2-2: THE FOUR FOUNDATIONS OF MINDFULNESS

---

[7] The linkages are shown in the Appendix to this Chapter.

	Table 2.5: MINDFUL ACCEPTANCE	
A	Attend to what arises	Maintaining a soft gaze to see the whole picture, accepting all that arises, and being open to new information.
C	Connect with it all	Connecting with everything that arises, including apparently opposite or conflicting views - aware that there is often more than one perspective. Open communication with others hearing what they say through dialogue.
C	Clear the mind of preconceptions	Keeping the mind open, willing to see everything as if for the first time. Allowing anything and everything that we experience from moment to moment to be here, because it already is. Aware of the possibility of what might arise, and reluctant to simplify interpretations, maintaining a suspicion of appearances.
E	Embody the experience	Integrating mind and body, reason and emotion.
P	Prevent premature judgement	Suspending judgement and waiting for the right moment.
T	Trust emergence	Taking responsibility for being yourself and learning to listen to and trust your own being.

Exhibit 5: COMMENTS OF PARTICIPANTS: ACCEPTANCE

- Acceptance of things as they are, things I can't change, only the way I deal with them.
- More able to support someone close to me who is having a difficult time - overcoming impatience and a need to control - able to show more acceptance, and compassion.
- Much better work life balance though still needs working on. More recognition that there is a choice about behaviour. More acceptance and less angst. Much more savouring.
- I find I'm more aware of taking time during the day to take a step back and reflect on what is going on around me. I also found it particularly useful and comforting, the idea of accepting negative thoughts and feelings, rather than trying to push them away.
- More tolerance, greater self-appreciation and appreciation of others. Got to confess I struggle a little with equanimity, but have been far more accepting of those who I feel have upset me or 'wronged me'.

As with Mindful Acceptance, an acronym integrates the various approaches summarised above, and thus characterise Mindful Change (Table 2.6).

Table 2.6: MINDFUL CHANGE		
C	Challenge preconceptions	Maintaining the soft gaze, maintaining suspicion of appearances even while acting decisively.
H.	Harmonise opposites	Seeking a balance of opposite views and perspectives, maintaining collaborative communication and dialogue.
A	Add new categories	Maintaining a reluctance to simplify interpretations, and an awareness of the possibility of what might be, and thereby willing to create new categories.
N	Notice what is happening	Maintaining attention, noticing what is really happening and staying open to new information. Paying serious attention to minute-to-minute operations and aware of imperfections in these activities. Striving to make ongoing assessments and continual updates.
G	Grow strengths and expertise	Developing one's strengths and addressing one's weaknesses, seeking to develop the Expert Mind, while remaining conscious of its dangers by maintaining also the Beginner's Mind.
E	Explore alternative perspectives	Continuing to explore all possibilities, including the views of others.

- (The course) introduced me to the idea of self-compassion and also seeing compassion in a much more individual way. So thinking of compassion toward your circle of friends and family and colleagues and people that I might meet. Also I suppose the notion that compassion is something that you can give to other people even if you don't know they're going to receive it. Whereas before it had been, there would be the people around me who more or less directly asked for it or I would feel sort of amorphous compassion to big issues around the world. So yes it changed it a huge amount.
- It can change the way you feel, cope and think.
- I have a new healthier perspective, and I am still noticing slight changes.
- The ongoing social support after the course (e.g. occasional emails/ social practice sessions) has enabled me to maintain changes 18 months after originally starting the course.

Between the two lies the mindful temporal space: *"A suspension of activity, a time or temporary disengagement when we are no longer moving toward any goal"* (Brach 2003:51). Although they have been presented here as distinct aspects, in practice these phases flow together, and the time involved in moving through all three may be very brief. Each supports and reinforces the other two.

MINDFUL LEARNING AND CBT: A COMPARISON

The inclusion of Mindful Learning in MBLE may be compared with the introduction of CBT into MBCT. Crane (2009) identifies five key elements, summarised in Table 2.7.

Table 2.7: COGNITIVE BEHAVIOURAL CURRICULUM COMPONENTS OF MBCT
Thoughts and feelings exercise
Learning about the territory of depression
Mood and alternative viewpoints exercise
Cognitive ways of working with difficult thoughts
Learning to see connections between activity and mood

All of these are used "to deepen insight into the nature of the mind" (Crane 2009:142). With the exception of the second, all these are addressed, albeit in different ways, by Mindful Learning. For example, the Mood and Alternative Viewpoints exercise helps participants recognise that "our interpretations are influenced by a number of things … they are not necessarily representations of the truth" (ibid:140), while the Thoughts and Feelings exercise helps us "see that our thoughts create a 'lens' through which we view the world" (ibid:138).

Mindful Learning has a broader compass. It reinforces the importance of the Beginner's Mind, and encourages an open approach to experience and learning. By way of example, I have used the three principles of the Pyrrhonist school - Suspicion of Appearances; Balancing of Opposite Views; and Suspension of Opinion - for many years on postgraduate research methods courses, as a way of encouraging students to take an open and sceptical stance in relation to their research.

As well as content, Crane sees the integration of CBT within MBCT as process, a distinctive learning environment which includes "movement within a mindfulness-based course from a deliberate and detailed engagement with personal experience, into a learning process that supports the participants in 'translating' this direct 'seeing' into learning" (ibid:151). Again, this parallels the role of Action Learning within the process of MBLE.

SUMMARY COMMENT

Mindfulness is obviously central to any MBI, and it is to be hoped that this chapter has demonstrated the value of including also the Western focus on mindful learning. They are complementary and strengthen each other. Now we widen the discussion to consider the value of extending the compass of MBIs.

3. THE FOUR IMMEASURABLES

In this chapter we explore the role of the Four Immeasurables – loving kindness, compassion, empathetic joy and equanimity – in Mindfulness Based Life Enhancement. We begin by looking at some of the problems which can arise when mindfulness is developed without the accompaniment of these qualities. We then explore each of them in more detail, and argue that there are many advantages in teaching them alongside mindfulness. They support mindfulness, and they also support each other.

INTRODUCTION

The Four Immeasurables are interrelated qualities, first identified 2500 years ago, but then detailed and systematised by Buddhaghosa (English translation 1956) in the fifth century CE. In this chapter we explore the case for their explicit role in Mindfulness Based Interventions, arguing that this can bring positive benefits to both mindfulness and to practitioners. This will be done in three parts. First, we consider the difficulties which can arise if mindfulness is not linked strongly to the Four Immeasurables. Second, we consider what each of the Four Immeasurables can contribute on their own, and third we consider their interrelationship - the argument here is that they mutually reinforce each other. They are thus more than the sum of their parts - they are a pattern that connects (Bateson 1973).

It is important to note at the outset that reservations about this **explicit** role of the qualities expressed in the Four Immeasurables are to be found in the literature: authors frequently reference expression of these qualities in facilitating an MBI course, seeing them as **implicit** to the activity. Thus Segal et al refer to gentleness and *"an attitude of caring to ourselves (whether an instructor or a participant)"* (2002:195), while Crane speaks of the need for teachers to *"bring gentleness and compassion to themselves and the participants"* (2009:158). Gilbert argues that *"compassion based therapists check carefully* *that whatever intervention they use … the person is able to do these in the spirit of validation, support and kindness"* (2010b:209).

Kabat-Zinn expresses reservation about taking this further: *"For a long time, I was reluctant to teach loving-kindness as a meditation practice in its own right"* (2005:285). In part this is because he sees all meditation as involving loving-kindness, in part because the embodiment of all four qualities in the practice means there is no need to be explicit, and mostly because it could be confusing to practitioners, with its sense of 'doing something'. Nonetheless the Stress Reduction Clinic does include formal loving-kindness practice during the all-day retreat "because of its potential to touch our hearts in such deep ways" (ibid:286). And in McCown et al's 'empty curriculum structure' for MBSR "cultivating kindness" is the explicit theme for week seven (2010:138). They recognise that the question of *"exactly how compassion-related practices should be integrated into a course devoted to the development of mindfulness skills has been a subject of debate in the MBSR community."* (2009:18). They report that in their own adaptations they incorporate all the Four Immeasurables.

There are other examples, such as the Mindfulness-Based Relationship Enhancement program developed by Carson et al (2004) in which mindfulness is seen as *"enhancing access to innate resources of joy, compassion and connectedness"* (472). For this they adapted MBSR to enhance the relationships of non-distressed couples, with *"greater emphasis on loving-kindness meditations"* (479), together with a variety of partner exercises. The conclusion of their research was that *"mindfulness was efficacious in enriching current relationship functioning and improving individual psychological well-being across a wide range of measures"* (488).

It has been suggested that mindfulness alone can lead to compassion. Thus MBSR has been proposed as an effective empathy-enhancing intervention (Block-Lerner et al. 2007; Shapiro and Izett 2008). But Birnie and colleagues (2010:368) argue that *"the inclusion of a directed empathy component (metta meditation) towards others may be key (Beddoe and Murphy 2004)".* Beddoe et al conclude: *"Addressing empathy indirectly (via mindfulness and self-care) may be less effective than more direct interventions."* (2004:309)

The question of how explicit, if at all, one should be about the Four Immeasurables in a Mindfulness Course can be considered in two ways. First, what are the possible consequences of focussing only on mindfulness? Second, what are the advantages of including these four values? We consider both questions. For the first, we look at some of the historical evidence of the misuse of mindfulness. One of the key sources of modern mindfulness is Zen practice, which has contributed much to the debate, as well as to the practice[8]. But the history of Zen has included a darker side, which can also teach us much. This discussion is expanded to look at the 'mindful sniper', and then at Zimbardo's characterisation of the Lucifer Effect. We will then turn to look at the positive benefits of integrating the Four Immeasurables with mindfulness.

MINDFULNESS WITHOUT THE FOUR IMMEASURABLES

THE DARK SIDE OF ZEN AT WAR

(Caution: This section, up to page 39, contains some distressing material.)

In the late 1990s two series of articles appeared in the Zen Quarterly, published by Sōtōshu Shumucho, the headquarters of SōtōZen in Japan. The first series related to the recall of one of the school's publications: "The History of Sōtō Zen Overseas Missionary Activities". Published in 1980, the History was recalled in 1993 and the journal articles are a critique of the role SōtōZen played in Imperial Japan, which had been reflected uncritically in the History, hence the recall.

One article summarises the position: *"Needless to add, Japan at that time (the period up to and including World War II) was dyed deeply by the colors of militarism. What is more, all the missionary activities of Buddhist religious organizations were extremely fascistic and sympathetic to national policies. In the School a mission system that was in total conformity with national policies*

---

[8] SōtōZen continues to be my primary practice, while Brian Victoria, whose critique is discussed below, is a SōtōZen ordained priest.

was accepted without the slightest suspicion. The attitude of the School at that time must naturally undergo criticism. It must be clearly defined as an error that should never be committed again. Nevertheless, the official history fails to criticize in any way the missionary activities of the Sōtō Zen School which sympathized, without question, with the national policies of that time" (Sōtōshu Shumucho 1998:2).

The articles argue that *"the Sōtō Zen School as a religious organization supported Japan's acts of aggression in China".* (1998:2) In particular, zazen became a tool of the military: *"Training" at that time meant the various activities to uphold and defend the national polity. In the School itself zazen was applied for this purpose of training. This meant that zazen was used in activities to protect the national polity in the military government of that time"* (Sōtōshu Shumucho 1999:7). However, while strongly condemnatory of what happened, the articles offer little by way of explanation as to why it happened.

The second series of articles concerned social discrimination in Sōtō Zen. The author, Bodiford, argues that *"Social discrimination against slaves, lepers, criminals, strangers, residents of undesirable areas, etc., has a long history in Japan. While scholars no longer believe that the origins of outcaste groups can be explained solely in terms of religious impurity (such as that resulting from the violation of taboos on animal butchering), appeals to religious sentiments certainly served to rationalize pre-existing prejudices. Buddhist doctrines of karmic retribution, in particular, suggest that disadvantaged people deserve their miserable fates"* (Bodiford 1997: 13).

Here there is some explanation - a distortion of the dharma - but a deeper analysis comes from Victoria's analysis of Zen at War (2006). Victoria examines Japanese Zen and its relationship with state power, with samurai culture and with bushido, the way of the sword. For hundreds of years, Zen masters trained samurai warriors in meditation, teaching them enhanced concentration and willpower. Zen helped them face adversity and death with no hesitation, to be totally loyal and to act unimpeded by thinking. Key to this was the transformation of a metaphor - the sword which cuts through delusion - into something literal - the sword which destroys people.

While there have been some critiques of aspects of Victoria's work, his overall thesis has not been challenged, and indeed in the second edition he states that the book had led several Zen sects to join the SōtōZen School in denouncing their previous activity. But of particular relevance to the present discussion are the explanations he gives for what happened. In addition to the close relationship between Buddhist hierarchy and state hierarchy, there were crucially a number of ways in which Buddhist teaching and practice was recast to fit a militaristic and imperialist agenda. One example is de-individuation, a corruption of no-self. Thus Zenkai, the administrative head of SōtōZen, wrote in 1941: "The essence of the practice of an (imperial) subject is to be found in the basic principle of the Buddha Way, which is to forget the self. It is by giving concrete form to this essence in any and all situations, regardless of time or place, that Buddhism is, for the first time, able to repay the debt of gratitude it owes to the state" (quoted in Victoria 2006:131).

Of most relevance to the present discussion is the treatment given to compassion. Victoria shows that compassion was not neglected during the period he analyses: rather, it was systematically distorted and corrupted. This is illustrated in several of the texts he quotes. Thus Sugimoto stated: *"The wars of the empire are sacred wars. They are holy wars. They are the (Buddhist) practice of great compassion"* (ibid 119). And Hayashiya and Shimakage, two SōtōZen scholars, argued in "The Buddhist View of War" that *"Japanese Buddhists believe that war conducted for a (good) reason is in accord with the great benevolence and compassion of Buddhism"* (quoted in Victoria 2006: 87).

This corruption began well before the outbreak of World War II. Thus in 1937, during what is now known as the rape of Nanking, *"Japanese soldiers butchered between 260,000 and 350,000 Chinese civilians in just a few bloody months … Chinese men were used for bayonet practice and in decapitation contests. An estimated 20,000 to 80,000 women were raped. Many soldiers went beyond rape to disembowel women, slice off their breasts, and nail them to walls alive. Fathers were forced to rape their daughters and sons their mothers as other family members watched"* (Zimbardo 2007:16-17). Here are the comments made by Zen scholar-priest Kodo that same year in an article entitled "The China Incident and Buddhism": *"Wherever the imperial military advances there is only charity and love. They could never act in the barbarous and cruel way in which the Chinese soldiers act. This can truly be considered to be a great accomplishment of the long period which Buddhism took in nurturing (the Japanese military). In other words, brutality itself no longer exists in the officers and men of the imperial military who have been schooled in the spirit of Buddhism"* (quoted in Victoria 2006:133).

Inoue Enryo, the noted Meiji-period Buddhist scholar-priest, had this to say shortly before the formal outbreak of hostilities: *"Buddhism is a teaching of compassion, a teaching for living human beings. Therefore, fighting on behalf of living human beings is in accord with the spirit of compassion. In the event hostilities break out between Japan and Russia, it is only natural that Buddhists should fight willingly, for what is this if not repaying the debt of gratitude we owe the Buddha?"* (quoted in Victoria 2006:29).

Victoria also cites the writings of Yasutani: *"It was in the same year that his complete enlightenment was confirmed, 1943, that Yasutani addressed the following comments to Japanese soldiers and civilians alike: What should the attitude of disciples of the Buddha, as Mahaayaana Bodhisattvas, be toward the first precept that forbids the taking of life? For example, what should be done in the case in which, in order to remove various evil influences and benefit society, it becomes necessary to deprive birds, insects, fish, etc. of their lives, or, on a larger scale, to sentence extremely evil and brutal persons to death, or for the nation to engage in total war? Those who understand the spirit of the Mahaayaana precepts should be able to answer this question immediately. That is to say, of course one should kill, killing as many as possible. One should, fighting hard, kill everyone in the enemy army. . . . Failing to kill an evil man who ought to be killed, or destroying an enemy army that ought to be destroyed, would be to betray compassion and filial obedience, to break the precept forbidding the taking of life"* (Victoria c2000).

In an interview with the New York Times *"Mr. Victoria said that imperial military trainers developed the self-denying egolessness Zen prizes into "a form of fascist mind-control." He said Suzuki and others helped by "romanticizing" the* tie between Zen and the warrior ethos of the samurai. Worse, he charges, they stressed a connection between Buddhist compassion and the acceptance of death in a way that justified collective martyrdom and killing one's enemies. In Islam, as in the holy wars of Christianity, there is a promise of eternal life," Mr. Victoria said in an interview. "In Zen, there was the promise that there was no difference between life and death, so you really haven't lost anything" (Jalon 2003).

Central to this approach was the practice of zazen, which was seen as "a unique methodology for the training of imperial subjects … Zazen was used not only to train officers and soldiers but also workers in war-industry factories. The training sessions were held either in the factory dormitory or in a nearby Zen temple, and they lasted for up to one week" (Victoria 2006:144).

One of the very few Japanese Zen priests to resist the imperial agenda was Gudō, who demonstrated the importance of embracing all beings when he wrote in 1907: "As a propagator of Buddhism I teach that "all sentient beings have the Buddha nature" and that "within the Dharma there is equality, with neither superior nor inferior." Furthermore, I teach that "all sentient beings are my children." Having taken these golden words as the basis of my faith, I discovered that they are in complete agreement with the principles of socialism. It was thus that I became a believer in socialism." (quoted in Victoria 2006:41) As Victoria comments: "The phrase, "all sentient beings have the Buddha-nature" is one of the central themes of the Lotus Sutra, as is the phrase, "all sentient beings are my children." The phrase, "within the Dharma there is equality, with neither superior or inferior" comes from the Diamond Sutra. Regrettably, this brief statement is the only surviving example of Gudō's understanding of the social implications of the Law of the Buddha" (ibid.).

Gudō's reward was to be condemned by the Zen hierarchy, and then in 1911 executed for high treason. In 1993, the Sōtō Zen sect restored Gudō's status as a priest saying that "when viewed by today's standards of respect for human rights, Uchiyama Gudō's writings contain elements that should be regarded as farsighted" and that "the sect's actions strongly aligned the sect with an establishment dominated by the emperor system. They were not designed to protect the unique Buddhist character of the sect's priests" (ibid.:47).

THE DARK SIDE OF ZEN IN PEACE

Victoria notes that this approach to Zazen persisted beyond the Second World War, in corporate Japan: *"Discipline, obedience, conformity and physical and mental endurance in the face of hardship are not the only features of monastic life attractive to corporate Japan. The traditional Buddhist teaching of the non-substantiality of the self has also been given a unique corporate twist … well illustrated by Ozeki Soen, the abbot of Rinzai Zen-sect affiliated Daisen'in temple: 'At every time and in every place, you should work selflessly' "* (2006:184-5). And Victoria adds: *"There is one further aspect of Zen training that is very attractive to corporate Japan, the practice of zazen itself. The samadhi power supposedly derived from the practice of zazen was originally utilized in Zen training to give the practitioner a deeper insight into his or her own nature and the nature of reality itself. Yet this same power, facilitating as it does complete absorption into the present moment, can be applied to any work, from wielding a samurai sword with lightning swiftness, to fighting selflessly on the battlefield, to manufacturing computer components with flawless precision"* (ibid:186).

WEGO

Discrimination and de-individuation are important factors in these accounts, and Loy's concept of the 'wego' helps explain what happens. He argues (Loy 2006) that as social beings, we tend to create collective senses of self, a 'wego', or group ego. We create collective identities based on race, class, gender, nation, religion, or some combination of these. In each case, the wego is created by discriminating one's own group from another. Loy explores this in his discussion of King's (1994) work "Zen and the Way of the Sword: Arming the Samurai Psyche": *"King identifies an inbuilt factor in Buddhism which tended to work against its own teaching that life is sacred: a doctrine of karmic destiny. And free as Zen may have been in some respects from the bonds of the Buddhist tradition, it was not free from the bonds of the teaching of karma"* (Loy 1995:278).

Loy goes on to suggest that this may help explain *"the recent scandals in many U.S. Zen centers, whose teachers (mostly Japanese or Japanese-trained) were discovered to have engaged in sexual, financial and other misconduct. If King is right, the basic difficulty is that Zen training does not in itself prepare such teachers to deal with the kinds of moral dilemmas and temptations that their positions expose them to, especially in a more individualistic, non-Confucian society"* (Loy 1995:280).

THE MINDFUL SNIPER: BARE AWARENESS IN THE MILITARY

The dangers of mindfulness without the balance of the Four Immeasurables can be further illustrated by the concept of the Mindful Sniper. Wallace has argued that: "A sniper hiding in the grass, waiting to shoot his enemy, may be quietly aware of whatever arises with each passing moment. But because he is intent on killing, he is practising wrong mindfulness. In fact, what he's practising is bare attention without an ethical component." For this reason it is important to avoid seeing mindfulness as comprising only bare attention, which otherwise "can easily lead to the misconception that the cultivation of mindfulness has nothing to do with ethics or with the cultivation of wholesome states of mind and the attenuation of unwholesome states. Nothing could be further from the truth" (2008:1).

Ricard supported this view during the Mind and Life conference in Dharamsala, April 2009: "The very fact of being mindful is just a very fine-tuned tool that can then readily be used for all sorts of purposes. The example of the sniper - they get in the flow, they enjoy it. And we cannot say this is contributing to wholesomeness. Like a hammer can be used for building or destroying, the motivation has to be the final factor to determine whether the mindfulness is wholesome or not." [9]

The nature of bare attention in military settings is explored by Harari in his study of Combat Flow (2008). He employs Csikszentmihalyi's (1990) concept of flow, and cites the combat experience of Shawn Nelson, an American soldier, in Mogadishu in 1993: *"Close to death, he had never felt so completely alive. . . . The only thing he could compare it to was the feeling he found sometimes when*

---

[9] Video extract available at http://www.youtube.com/watch?v=_NKlHGCFiYM

he surfed, when he was inside the tube of a big wave and everything around him was energy and motion and he was being carried along by some terrific force and all he could do was focus intently on holding his balance, riding it out. Surfers called it The Green Room. Combat was another door to that room. A state of complete mental and physical awareness. In those hours on the street he had not been Shawn Nelson, he had no connection to the larger world, no bills to pay, no emotional ties, nothing. He had just been a human being staying alive from one nano-second to the next, drawing one breath after another, fully aware that each one might be his last. He felt he would never be the same" (Bowden, 2001, pp. 301, 302).

Harari argues that in combat *"one's entire awareness is absorbed in the present moment"* (2008:254). He connects this to three other characteristics: first, excluding all irrelevant thoughts; second, becoming fully concentrated in the present; and third, *"an exhilarating and heightened sense of being alive"*. Thus he quotes another veteran Ben-Yehuda, who explained that "the best thing about war is that in war, *"we have only the present"*. And all this enables combat soldiers to *"maximize their mental and physical abilities."* (ibid)

THE LUCIFER EFFECT

We can take this discussion further by considering the findings of social psychology in relation to the processes taking place in organisations. Power and influence are pervasive in most areas of human interaction. Here we approach the subject by considering three interrelated aspects:

- The sources of power
- The processes by which power is exercised
- The content involved, in particular values, norms, and ideologies, leading to particular outcomes.

In 1960 French and Raven identified five sources of power; subsequent writers have extended the list, and more recently Nye (2004) has developed the distinction between hard and soft power (Table 3.1). In the dark sides of

Zen discussed earlier all these sources - reward, coercive, legitimate, expert, referent, information and connection - are manifest.

Table 3.1: HARD AND SOFT POWER		
Hard Power	Reward Power	Can influence the rewards given to others: tangible (e.g. money, awards) or intangible (e.g. status, compliments).
	Coercive Power	Can inflict punishments whether tangible (e.g. physical injury, withheld resources) or not (e.g. slights, demotion).
	Legitimate Power	Invocation of rank, title to compel others to act or gain compliance.
Soft Power	Expert Power	Holds special knowledge or expertise on which others depend.
	Referent Power	Ability to inspire people to follow your example, often called charisma
	Information Power	Has access to or holds non-public information.
	Connection Power	Results from personal and professional access to key people inside and outside the organisation.
Sources: First five from French, J. P. R. Jr., and Raven, B. (1960). The Bases of Social Power.		
In D. Cartwright and A. Zander (eds.), Group Dynamics (pp. 607-623). New York: Harper and Row.		

In the field of social psychology there has been extensive exploration of the use and abuse of power, summarised by Zimbardo as the 'Lucifer Effect' (2007). His analysis ranges from the Stanford Prison Experiment (which he led) to the Abu Ghraib abuses (he appeared as an expert witness for an American soldier jailed for these abuses). His concern is to understand why ordinary people can commit evil acts: he argues that *"people's character may be transformed by their being immersed in situations that unleash powerful situational forces"* (2007:8), and this relates to both process and content.

The key processes involve the ways in which people's behaviour can change through peer pressure, in particular where there is a desire to be accepted by the group. This leads to conformity to group norms. Behaviour can also change due to obedience to authority. These are two examples of the way influence occurs; Cialdini, who has reviewed the many social psychology experiments that have taken place, extends this to six (Table 3.2).

Table 3.2: INFLUENCE AND PERSUASION	
Reciprocity	The rule of reciprocity requires that one person try to repay, in kind, what another person has provided
Consistency and Commitment	People desire to look consistent within their words, beliefs, attitudes, and deeds
Social Validation	People determine what is correct by finding out what other people think is correct
Liking	People prefer to say "yes" to individuals they know and like
Authority	Milgram's studies of obedience provide evidence of a strong pressure for compliance with the requests of authority figures
Scarcity	People assign more value to opportunities when they are less available if there are fewer resources and less time to get them, we want it more
Cialdini, R B (2001) Harnessing the Power of Persuasion HBR Oct	

These processes push people to act in certain ways; they also prevent action. Zimbardo points to "the evil of inaction: passive bystanders" (2007:317), who do not intervene, and thereby allow evil to persist, something manifest in recent Zen scandals, as well as other religious scandals such as child abuse in the Catholic church.

We can enrich this debate by adding Lukes' analysis of power in three dimensions (2005). The first dimension is overt power - A influences the behaviour of B. The second dimension is where A defines the agenda, using both hard and soft power: "the power to decide what is decided "(ibid.:111). In both these dimensions the influence is clear and external.

The third dimension is where A shapes the preferences of B through values, norms, ideologies. Here the influence is internalised - B accepts these values as their own, and acts accordingly. *"Is it not the supreme and most insidious exercise of power to prevent people, to whatever degree, from having grievances by shaping their perceptions, cognitions and preferences in such a way that they accept their role in the existing order of things, either because they can see or imagine no alternative to it, or because they see it as natural and unchangeable, or because they value it as divinely ordained and beneficial?"* (ibid:28)

Turning to the third aspect of power, content, Zimbardo explores the values, norms, and ideologies which lead to evil, and foremost amongst these are deindividuation and dehumanisation. This was summarised in a BBC documentary Five Steps to Tyranny[10], which drew on social psychology experiments as well as evidence from Kosovo, Burma, Israel/Palestine, Rwanda and Bosnia. After creating 'us' and 'them', the power-brokers insist everyone obeys their orders. The enemy - 'them' - is dehumanised, and followers are told to 'stand up' or 'stand by', thereby suppressing dissent and opposing opinions. The final step is action against 'them' - discrimination, abuse, even ethnic cleansing.

The discussion above illuminates the issues raised earlier, for we can see that both soft and hard power were used

- To induce conformity and obedience to authority
- By exercising power and influence at both the second (external) and third (internalised) dimensions

---

[10] Available at http://www.youtube.com/watch?v=rmDQPUx1Pj8

- To induce deindividuation and dehumanisation, and thereby facilitate abuse, discrimination and atrocity.

The atrocities committed by Japanese soldiers were willingly done because they had internalised a belief system which potentially embraced their own suicide - the third dimension of power. The individual soldier was deindividuated. Social discrimination occurred because the 'outcasts' were dehumanised. Bandura (2006:225) has argued that ideology frequently drives inhumanity, and involves moral disengagement, so that "people who behave compassionately in other areas of their lives can perpetrate ruthless inhumanities on disfavored groups." He identified eight mechanisms that people use to rationalize immoral behaviour (Table 3.3.) Although his studies have not included the issues discussed above, the eight mechanisms have a chilling resonance.

Table 3.3: MECHANISMS PEOPLE USE TO RATIONALISE IMMORAL BEHAVIOUR	
Moral justification	Soldiers learn to see killing in the context of a larger good; terrorists may say they are punishing "nonbelievers."
Euphemistic labelling	"Collateral damage"; "clean, surgical strikes"; and having someone "taken care of" are all familiar examples.
Advantageous comparison	Comparing an enemy to Hitler to justify an attack; or excusing a reckless act by comparing it to worse transgression by a rival or predecessor.
Displacement of responsibility	Shifting the blame to a boss, a leader or another authority figure; "I was just carrying out orders."
Diffusion of responsibility	Sharing the responsibility for a transgression with others who took part, or who played indirect roles: "Everyone was doing it."

Disregard or distortion of consequences	Refusal to acknowledge the reality of the damage caused; rationalizing that "it wasn't all that bad."
Dehumanization	Assailing others as degenerates, devils, savages or infidels. Some torturers refer to their victims as "worms."
Blaming the victim	The people being cheated or attacked are "asking for it."
Albert Bandura, Stanford University; Source: New York Times 7 February 2006 Accessed at: http://query.nytimes.com/gst/fullpage.html?res=9906E0 DA173EF934A35751C0A9609C8B63&pagewanted=all	

This discord between compassion and inhumanity is to be found even in music. Thus Goodall points out that compassion is central to Wagner's opera Parsifal: *"Compassion, the piece teaches, has a healing and liberating power"* (2013:198). But the villain of the piece, Klingsor *"was typically portrayed in Parsifal productions as of Arabic or Jewish origin"* (ibid:201), just one example of the composer's extreme anti-Semitism, bringing Hitler to proclaim *"I intend to base my religion on the Parsifal legend"*. As Goodall concludes *"In one way, this became the most dangerous music ever written, because, despite being motivated by a devotion to self-denial and compassion, it undoubtedly inspired hatred"* (ibid:203).

CONCLUSIONS

We need to recognise that in people (and organisations) we find both positive and negative, a view given further support by research on the brain, which has led Armstrong to conclude that *"We are hard-wired for compassion as well as for cruelty"* (2011:14). As Chödrön says *"They aren't really opposed to each other ... The Buddha within is bad and good coexisting, evil and purity coexisting"* (1994:30-1). And this recognition that people have both positive and negative qualities has a very long history, in both Eastern and Western thinking. Flanagan, asking how it is possible for people to progress *"from a first nature partly constituted by the poisons to a second nature where these are quieted, quelled, or eliminated"* concludes *"The answer, similar to Mencius (the great Chinese philosopher), Aristotle, Hume and Darwin is that, in addition to the bad or destructive seeds or sprouts in our nature, there are also the seeds of fellow feeling, empathy, and compassion"* (2011:108).

There are a number of important conclusions to be drawn from the above discussion. Looking first to the Zen tradition, and Zen centres in both East and West, we need to recognise that they are as susceptible to corruption and malpractice as other organisations. Whether the malpractice involves violence, intimidation or sexual misconduct, the common factor is the pervasive role of power and influence. The abuse of power leads to conformity and obedience, exacerbated in Zen by the nature of the teacher-pupil relationship. As part of this abuse of power, Buddhist teachings such as no-self and karma can easily be distorted to fit harmful intentions. The Buddhist teachings on compassion are also open to distortion, primarily by being presented in a partial manner - compassion only for "us", and not "them". These distortions can lead to deindividuation and discrimination - two key factors in the generation of harmful activity, and they appear in many other settings, including organisations and societies. The passive bystander phenomenon is also evident in these settings.

Box 3: CROUCHING TIGERS, HIDDEN DRAGONS

The experience of another group process, Whole Systems Methodology[11], may be helpful here. In this a group of people with a common interest (ranging in size from 20 to 200) meet together to identify issues and develop an action strategy. It is an inclusive process involving individual, group and plenary work, and in the early stages usually generates considerable enthusiasm and energy as people explore possibilities.

---

[11] For further details on this, see Darwin, Johnson and McAuley 2002, Chapter 11.

But there is then the real possibility of a backlash, when people realised the scale of what may be involved, and retreat. Rather than allowing this to creep up on them, it is best to pre-empt the negative by moving from Practical Vision to Underlying Contradictions. In this stage, participants are specifically invited to identify the problems that may prevent them achieving the Practical Vision (the following stage is then work on addressing these problems). One way of doing this is to adopt the film metaphor of "Crouching Tigers, Hidden Dragons" - the Crouching Tigers are the difficulties which are easy to see, the Hidden Dragons are those lurking in the shadows. This has proved an effective way of keeping participants in control of the problems, rather than the reverse, and can be used also in MBLE, warning people that difficulties will arise, some easily identifiable, others coming as if from nowhere. The introduction of the Negativity Bias in the first week of the MBLE course is in part to prepare people for this.

There are problems in any form of 'bare awareness without an ethical component'. These include 'flow states' of complete mental and physical awareness. Since we are hard-wired for cruelty as well as compassion, the latter needs to be explicitly addressed and developed. Compassion needs the support of loving kindness, which "guards against turning into partiality, prevents compassion from making discriminations by selecting and excluding and thus protects it from falling into partiality or aversion against the excluded side" (Nyanaponika Thera 1994). It also needs the support of equanimity, addressing the dangers of preference and prejudice: "through equanimity, you develop composure, an internal calm that allows you to see into the working of things, to understand the situation, and to know what can or cannot be done" (McLeod 2001:299).

Therefore while loving-kindness and compassion should be explicitly addressed, so too should Joy and Equanimity. For example, compassion needs the support of equanimity, addressing the dangers of preference and prejudice. Altruistic/sympathetic/empathetic[12] joy links well with the stress in Mindfulness Based Life Enhancement on positive enhancement. **It is therefore essential to complement the practice of mindfulness with the Four Immeasurables.**

There is a caveat to this. It is worth emphasising once again that the argument in this book relates to non-clinical, non-therapeutic groups. Segal et al comment that *"Any kindness - even when embodied implicitly thought a compassionate and mindful presence in the classroom may have an impact on participants that is not uniformly positive. As a phenomenon, this is actually not that unusual when dealing with clinical populations"* (2013:142). They point to Germer's (2009) comment that *"when any of us start to show ourselves greater kindness we may also notice a rebound back into negative feelings, so that it is useful to prepare participants for moments when such bad feelings may arise. The skilful thing for an instructor to do is point this out without inducing undue pessimism"* (ibid:142-3).

COUNTERVAILING FORCES: THE FOUR IMMEASURABLES

Thus far the argument has been that there are strong situational and relational forces which can lead people into harmful behaviour, and that mindfulness on its own will not prevent this. It is time to be more positive, and we can begin with Zimbardo who invites readers to consider "whether you are capable of becoming a hero" (2007:21). He argues that people should become more mindful: "We need to be reminded not to live our lives on automatic pilot, but always to take a Zen moment to reflect on the meaning of the immediate situation, to think before acting" (2007:453). This has led Zimbardo to his 'heroic imagination' project. One of the key questions being asked in this project is: What is the role of compassion and empathy in heroism?[13]

---

[12] This Immeasurable is variously styled – partly through running MBLE I have now centred on Empathetic Joy since 'empathy' is a term which resonates with people

[13] http://heroicimagination.org/research/hip-research-questions/

The argument in this chapter is that the Four Immeasurables, together with mindfulness, can make a major contribution to this different learning, in particular through the practice given by Buddhaghosa (1956), involving multiple stages beginning with oneself and extending to include enemies and all sentient beings. It is important in this to embrace all Four Immeasurables - for example, equanimity provides an antidote to the 'us-them' divide - a divide which the Japanese experience shows can be integrated with compassion. McLeod comments that equanimity practice *"first exposes prejudices and then works to pry you loose from them"* (2001:264). And as Zimbardo argues, through mindfulness we can become alert to the nature and types of power present in a situation, including inappropriate use of authority, influence and persuasion. We can better resist the pressures to conformity. So mindfulness plus the Four Immeasurables can help us avoid the dangers of prejudice, discrimination and deindividuation. Gilbert and Choden put it this way: "When we do certain mindfulness and compassion exercises they tend to co-arise; that is, they tend also to build and support each other" (2013:118).

This means deeper consideration of the nature of the Four Immeasurables. There is disagreement whether they are emotions. Levine includes love and compassion as 'noble passions' (2009:37), but Ekman contends to the Dalai Lama that compassion is not an emotion, differing in four ways - it needs to be cultivated, it is enduring, it does not distort our perception of reality, and it is restricted to the relief of suffering (Ekman 2008:140-1). Ekman and the Dalai Lama (who sees compassion as 'a kind of emotion') do not resolve this in their debate, but what can be said is that their opposites are emotions, as can be seen by reviewing Goleman's families of emotions (Table 3.4).

Emotions are usually divided into two categories - positive and negative. But as Ekman argues there are problems "with such a simple dichotomy" (2003: 58-9). First it ignores important differences in the 'negative' emotions, and second these are not always experienced as unpleasant. It would seem better to think of emotions as harmful or beneficial, in terms of oneself and others, and recognise that many emotions can take either form, depending on the specific context. "Negative emotions serve a useful function by alerting us to a problem. ... We don't want to eliminate negative feelings, we just don't want to get stuck on them" (Germer 2009:117).

Table 3.4: THE BASIC FAMILIES OF EMOTIONS	
Fear (Safety)	anxiety, apprehension, nervousness, concern, consternation, misgiving, wariness, qualm, edginess, dread, fright, terror and in the extreme cases phobia and panic.
Anger (Justice)	fury, outrage, resentment, wrath, exasperation, indignation, vexation, acrimony, animosity, annoyance, irritability, hostility, and perhaps these are manifest in the extreme as hatred and violence.
Sadness (Loss)	grief, sorrow, cheerlessness, gloom, melancholy, self-pity, loneliness, dejection, despair, and depression in the extreme case.
Enjoyment (Gain)	happiness, joy, relief, contentment, bliss, delight, amusement, pride, sensual pleasure, thrill, rapture, gratification, satisfaction, euphoria, whimsy, ecstasy, and at the far edge, mania.
Love (Attraction)	acceptance, friendliness, trust, kindness, affinity, devotion, adoration, infatuation, and agape.
Disgust (Repulsion)	contempt, distain, scorn, abhorrence, aversion, distaste, and revulsion
Surprise (Attention)	shock, astonishment, amazement, and wonder
Shame(Self-Control)	embarrassment, chagrin, remorse, humiliation, regret, mortification, and contrition.
Daniel Goleman (1995) Emotional Intelligence Appendix "A"	

It is therefore helpful to address both the positive and the negative. As the Buddha put it: *"Energy will be set upon the abandoning of everything unwholesome and the acquiring of everything wholesome"* (Nyaponika Thera and Bhikkhu Bodhi 2007:157). We are therefore fully accepting here the argument of Flanagan that *"Reference to virtues and vices, and to the aim of trying to equip agents with a good character comprised of virtues is psychologically, sociologically, and politically wise, as well as ontologically respectable"* (2011:146). He defines a virtue as a disposition (to perceive and/or to feel and/or to think and/or to judge and/or to act) in a way that is appropriate to the situation; it is "a reliable habit of the heart-mind" (ibid:150).

It is in this spirit that we now explore the Four Immeasurables, which are considered by Buddhism to be the four highest emotions. These four qualities are closely related, as characterised in the description of the link between mother and child.

Box 4: MOTHER AND CHILD

Loving-Kindness is seen in the bond between a mother and her newborn child.

Compassion is seen in this same mother child relationship which remains undisturbed by fear when the child is suffering.

Empathetic Joy is expressed in this relationship when the child begins to express their own creative nature. It is the ability to join and support this expanding spirit.

Equanimity is seen as the child leaves home. With a heart full of good will, compassion and appreciative joy we stand at the threshold of their departure.

One of Buddhagosa's many important contributions to the development of the Four Immeasurables was his identification of the Near Enemies and the Far Enemies. Each Immeasurable has a Near Enemy, a deceptive substitute which we can settle for or confuse with the real thing. This can separate us from the true feeling, rather than connecting us to it, so we need mindfulness to avoid it.

Each Immeasurable also has a direct opposite, its Far Enemy – many of which are to be found also in Table 3.4. Developing the Four Immeasurables helps us to challenge these in ourselves.

Table 3.5: THE NEAR AND FAR ENEMIES		
	Near Enemy	Far Enemy
LOVING KINDNESS	Attachment, greed	Hatred, ill will
COMPASSION	Pity, grief	Cruelty
EMPATHETIC JOY	Joy tinged with insincerity or personal identification; forms of joy that are excessive such as elation, exuberance; Schadenfreude	Envy, jealousy, Aversion
EQUANIMITY	Indifference, foolish unknowing	Greed, taking of sides, partiality, resentment, reactivity

LOVING KINDNESS

Loving-kindness is a genuine feeling of caring and respect for others. We wish them to be happy and to have whatever they need for a healthy, satisfying life. This is a feeling of caring and kindness. It doesn't mean that we must have a close relationship. It means we care about that person, appreciate what they do for us and wish them happiness.

Loving kindness is a heartfelt desire that others might experience happiness and the sources of happiness. It involves engaging with the subjective reality of another person, with their joys and sorrow, hopes and fears, similar to our own, and then wishing that they, like us, may be happy. This can start in mindfulness practice.

The Far Enemy of Loving Kindness is hatred, ill will and anger. These can take many forms including self-judgement. The near enemy of loving-kindness is attachment, greed and conditional love. We have all noticed how attachment can creep into our love relationships. True love is an expression of openness: "I love you as you are without any expectations or demands." Attachment has in it a sense of separation: "Because you are separate from me, I need you." At first, attachment may feel like love, but as it grows it becomes more clearly the opposite, characterised by clinging, controlling, and fear.

Wallace relates loving kindness to the pursuit of happiness. Noting that many thinkers – such as Saint Augustine, William James and the Dalai Lama - have said that this is the purpose of life, he argues that *they are obviously referring to something more than the pursuit of mere pleasant stimulation. They have in mind something deeper. … Genuine happiness is a symptom of a balanced, healthy mind, just as a sense of physical well-being is a sign of a healthy body*" (2006:170). This involves escaping the hedonic treadmill, and "the first step to escaping from this exhausting grind is to seek a vision of genuine happiness that draws on our own, largely untapped inner resources. This is how we begin to cultivate loving-kindness first for ourselves, and then for all those around us" (ibid:26).

Emotional contagion is relevant here. The negative aspects of this were seen in the riots in several parts of England in 2011, but there are many positive examples. Happiness itself is contagious. Fowler and Christakis report that *"People who are surrounded by many happy people and those who are central in the network are more likely to become happy in the future. Longitudinal statistical models suggest that clusters of happiness result from the spread of happiness and not just a tendency for people to associate with similar individuals*" (2008:23). This includes smiling[14], and MBLE includes a smiling meditation which invariably proves very popular.

---

[14] "Why it is hard to keep a straight face" Accessed at http://news.bbc.co.uk/1/hi/sci/tech/2349981.stm

COMPASSION

Compassion is the feeling which arises when we regard all beings (beginning with oneself and one's own family and friends but not stopping there) with loving-kindness but then perceive the universal experience of suffering. Compassion is associated with a sense of commitment, responsibility, and respect towards all other people. As Gilbert and Choden put it: *"Compassion needs to be understood as consisting of multiple attributes and skills, and yet holding to the fact that at its core is motivation: the desire for all living things to be free of suffering and the causes of suffering"* (2013:98).

With compassion we want others not to have pain, problems or unhappiness. Compassion comes from realizing that they suffer. Our own experiences of suffering are the basis for compassion. We know what it's like to be sick or in pain, to be lonely or have our feelings hurt by an unkind remark, to fear the unknown or mourn the death of a loved one. When we then see or hear of others experiencing these things, our heart opens with a feeling of empathy and a wish to help.

The Far Enemy of Compassion is cruelty. Cruelty is devoid of mercy. Compassion practice is a safe way to expose latent cruelty that may exist at an unconscious level. The Near Enemy of compassion is pity and grief, and these also separate us. Pity feels sorry for "that poor person over there," as if they were somehow different from us, whereas true compassion is the resonance of our heart with the suffering of another. "Yes, I, too, together with you, share in the sorrows of life."

Paul Gilbert, who has recently developed Compassion Focused Therapy, sees the essence of compassion as *"a basic kindness, with a deep awareness of the suffering of oneself and of other living things, coupled with the wish and effort to relieve it"* (2010a:13). It is important to stress here that compassion, like all the Four Immeasurables, is to be found in many traditions. Thus it is often linked to the Golden Rule[15]. Flanagan comments *"The love required by Jesus*

---

[15] http://en.wikipedia.org/wiki/Golden_Rule and http://www.humanismforschools.org.uk/pdfs/the%20golden%20rule.pdf

in the Golden Rule is decidedly not personal love in any of the familiar forms; it is not romantic or sibling or parental or communal love. It is best described as compassion or loving-kindness toward anyone and everyone who suffers. As I understand Buddhism, it recommends the same virtues, the same kind of love" (2011:199).

Exhibit 7: COMMENTS OF PARTICIPANTS: COMPASSION

- The loving kindness and compassionate meditations have been very supportive and are enabling me to express joy and gratefulness to people around me, especially in my relationship.
- I have found incorporating loving kindness and compassion to all things in my daily life extremely helpful, both in my work and in my personal life. It has been transformative in my relationship with my son.
- Reflecting upon compassion and joy are perhaps the two most memorable aspects for me. Too often I feel over sensitive about aspects of everyday life - e.g. when I see hardship and suffering. To reflect on compassion, helps me release some of the 'guilt' and see how to focus my mind more positively. To help bring joy where possible.
- A heightened awareness. A recognition that we are all souls journeying through life and trying to make sense of it - and that therefore we should feel compassionately towards our fellow travellers. A sense of calm, and of time slowing down.

Empathetic Joy and Equanimity are the least stressed of the Four Immeasurables in discussions of mindfulness, and it is therefore useful to explore them in some depth. Nyaponika Thera argues that Empathetic Joy – mudita - "has not received sufficient attention either in expositions of Buddhist ethics, or in the meditative development of the four sublime states of which mudita is one."[16] He recognises the difficulties of identifying with the joys of others, but suggests it may have roots even deeper than compassion, in our gregarious and cooperative nature.

With empathetic joy we wish all beings to have pure happiness. This means taking delight in others' success, good qualities and positive actions, and rejoicing in their joy. It brings us closer to others. Empathetic joy means truly rejoicing with another person in all that is good and going well in their life. It means enjoyment at the sight of others who have attained happiness. As Salzberg says: *"It is a rare and beautiful quality to feel truly happy when others are happy. When someone rejoices in our happiness, we are flooded with respect and gratitude for their appreciation. When we take delight in the happiness of another, when we genuinely rejoice at their prosperity, success, or good fortune rather than begrudging it in any way, we are abiding in sympathetic joy"* (1995:151).

Wallace describes it as follows: *"The cultivation of empathetic joy involves attending closely to something that is already a reality, the joys, success and virtues of yourself and others. Empathy is feeling with others, and in this practice we focus not on their sorrows and difficulties, but on their happiness and triumphs. This practice is a direct antidote to feelings of depression, anxiety and hopelessness that may arise in the course of meditation or simply in the course of daily living"* (2006:57-8).

Natasha Jackson argues for the general relevance of empathetic joy ('mudita'): *"To regard mudita as being relevant only on certain relatively rare occasions*

[16]Source: http://www.accesstoinsight.org/lib/authors/various/wheel170.html accessed 14.12.2012

when our friends and acquaintances come into a bonanza of some kind, is to fragment it and render it trivial, thereby missing the essential matrix. It should not be regarded as a matter of turning on a tap from which mudita will gush forth. There should be, in a certain sense, a quiet stream of sympathy and understanding flowing within the individual all the time. Though, to be sure, it does also mean developing the capacity to participate in another person's finest hour and doing so spontaneously and sincerely. It is indeed a depressing fact that people are much more ready to sympathize with the misfortunes of others than to rejoice with them, a psychological quirk in people which wrung from Montaigne the ironic statement: 'There is something altogether not too displeasing in the misfortunes of our friends"(undated[17]).

It is not only the misfortune of friends which can easily arouse pleasure. Consider for example the temptation to indulge in 'schadenfreude' - "pleasure derived from the misfortunes of others" - which is often the root of comedy, ranging from Shakespeare's Caliban and other fools, to episodes of Seinfeld. In the latter, George "experiences momentary elation, especially when he has achieved some victory over others." But this never lasts "because George's personality will always intervene eventually". And that personality is characterised by him hating himself, his inability to interact with women, his boring life, his weak-willed nature (Barwick 2000:21-23). The extent to which comedy depends on the misfortune of others is a sobering realisation.

The Far Enemies of Empathetic Joy are envy, jealousy, and aversion. The Near Enemies of empathetic joy include hedonism and, of course, schadenfreude.

Like Nyaponika Thera, Jackson suggests that *"Mudita is one of the most neglected topics within the whole range of the Buddha Dhamma, probably because of its subtlety and of the wealth of nuances latent within it."*[18] The same applies in the literature on Mindfulness Based Interventions - while the other three qualities receive extensive treatment, empathetic joy rarely does. However, perhaps influenced by the rise of positive psychology, there has been a growing

---

[17] Accessed at http://www.accesstoinsight.org/lib/authors/various/wheel170.html

[18] Accessed at http://www.accesstoinsight.org/lib/authors/various/wheel170.html

emphasis in recent years on the positive, in particular on happiness, and this is to be found also in Buddhist texts (e.g. Dalai Lama and Cutler 1999, Ricard 2007). This is explored further in the next chapter.

MBLE participants characterise Empathetic Joy well:

- Being in someone else's shoes, resonating with somebody else's feelings
- You have to really and sincerely feel happy for other people's achievements
- You can rejoice in somebody else's gain or success
- Being pleased when other people are taking pleasure in their happiness
- It makes you feel happy as well when other people are happy, when your friends are happy, it rubs off on you.

We can extend this discussion to consider the distinction between Eudaimonia and Hedonism, and suggest that the focus here is on eudaimonic happiness: "Eudaimonia is a Greek word commonly translated as happiness or welfare; however, "human flourishing" has been proposed as a more accurate translation"[19]. "The concept of *eudaimonia,* a key term in ancient Greek moral philosophy, is … standardly translated as "happiness" or "flourishing" and occasionally as "well-being.""[20]

By contrast, "Hedonism is a school of thought that argues that pleasure is the only intrinsic good. In very simple terms, a hedonist strives to maximize net pleasure (pleasure minus pain). Ethical hedonism is the idea that all people have the right to do everything in their power to achieve the greatest amount of pleasure possible to them."[21] "Motivational hedonism is the claim that only pleasure or pain motivates us. It is the most significant form of psychological hedonism. Normative hedonism is the claim that all and only pleasure has worth or value, and all and only pain has disvalue."[22] Hedonism is sometimes characterised as a treadmill in which our desire for more – whether possessions or experiences – becomes a neverending cycle (Figure 3-1).

---

[19]Source http://en.wikipedia.org/wiki/Eudaimonia accessed 14.12.2012l
[20]Source http://plato.stanford.edu/entries/ethics-virtue/#2
[21]Source http://en.wikipedia.org/wiki/Hedonism
[22]Source http://en.wikipedia.org/wiki/Hedonism

Exhibit 8: COMMENTS OF PARTICIPANTS: EMPATHETIC JOY

- Enjoying the pleasures of life more. Rushing around less - being a bit more laid back and philosophical about deadlines. Try to focus on what I am doing in the moment and not stress about work I have not yet done.
- Pausing and acknowledging when I am enjoying something, something good is happening. Taking more time to enjoy simple pleasures in life. Stopping myself when I am caught up in something negative that has happened. Acknowledge but try not to let negatives take over when there are positives.
- I would like to think I've always been pretty compassionate, kind and joyful. But the course has helped me focus on those qualities, and try and understand things from another's point of view.
- Hard to know where to start. Freer. More confident, more solid, more curious about myself and my feelings and thoughts and delighted to recognise them and own them and have more strength and more strategies to work with them even when really difficult, destructive, negative and strong. More patient with self and others. More tolerant and respectful of self and others. Kinder. More appreciative of self and others. Enjoy life more. More adventurous!
- Resolved to focus on bringing more joy into my life.

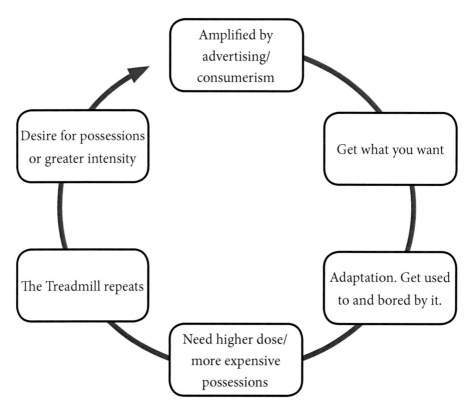

FIGURE 3-1: THE HEDONIC TREADMILL

This distinction between Eudaimonia and Hedonism also allows us to link Empathetic Joy with Gratitude. Thus respondents commented on the latter:

- I like to be grateful at every moment and every day and at every moment I need to remember to be grateful.
- I suddenly felt so happy and grateful for everything.
- I especially liked the exercise about gratitude sort of thinking about quite small things but also the huge pleasure then you can get from being grateful for small things and that's made me feel much more appreciative particularly of nature.

EQUANIMITY

With equanimity we have equal respect and concern for every being regardless of where they stand in relation to us. Equanimity is a perfect, unshakable balance of mind, rooted in insight. Looking at the world around us, and looking into our own heart, we see clearly how difficult it is to attain and maintain balance of mind. Equanimity means a balanced state of mind, through which we are able to contemplate by focusing the mind between the two extremes of attachment and indifference.

The Far Enemies of Equanimity are greed, resentment and partiality. Equanimity is the capacity to let go, to let be. The Near Enemy of equanimity is indifference. True equanimity is balance in the midst of experience, whereas indifference is a withdrawal and not caring. It is to be noted that the balance sought in equanimity does not necessarily involve equality. The research done on the negativity bias[23] demonstrates how easy it is to allow the negative to outweigh the positive, even when the latter predominates. Equanimity is therefore is in part about achieving balance - seek three goods to each bad experienced!

Equanimity is the feeling of even-mindedness in the face of both suffering and joy. It is the ability to be equal minded in all circumstances and towards everyone. For Wallace: *"The essence of equanimity is impartiality. It is equanimity that allows loving-kindness, compassion, and empathetic joy to expand boundlessly. Normally, these qualities are mixed with attachment, but we grow beyond the mental affliction of attachment as we realize that every sentient being is equally worthy of finding happiness and freedom from suffering"* (2006:69).

---

[1] Explored in the next Chapter.

- All kinds of prejudice should be eliminated from our thoughts and our minds and our actions because prejudice actually will come in so many different shapes and meanings.
- A real passion and concern for justice. For justice that extends to all people.
- As human beings we all have rights, the right for a peaceful life, for justice.
- That is kind of feeling balance.
- I experience equanimity as a space where I am approaching the situations as if for the first time, so I am not going in with my head full of assumptions or prejudices or ideas about how it's going to be or how I wanted to be. It's a non-judgmental attitude which opens me up to the bigger picture, it enables me to hold polarities and be open to different perspectives.
- Generally I learnt about 'The near enemy'- this is a very powerful language and concept. Specifically - Equanimity - I am getting better at letting things be, I think this too shall pass, or "that's just how it is right now." With the other three I am still very much learning - a lifetime of patterns to undo!! But at least now I have some insight into what I want to be like, and I do try and live this way e.g. if I compare myself or my 'lot' with someone else and find myself feeling irritated (i.e. envious or ' it's not fair') now I will consciously tell myself not to think X&Y, but rather to think that that person is striving to get their needs met, just like me.
- During a close relative's hospital stay I tried to see things from his point of view (as he refused treatment to save his life). Obviously we were panicking but I tried to be calm for him and not put all my panic onto him as well. He did survive but it was very close and I found it hard to accept he did not want to live - my instinct was to plead and later be angry - but I tried to bring a bit of equanimity to bear. Now we are out of the crisis I am reviewing the whole period in the light of the qualities which helps put things in a calmer light.

Fronsdal and Pandita (2005:40) have developed the Buddhist concept of equanimity in a way that is helpful here, arguing that *"while some may think of equanimity as dry neutrality or cool aloofness, mature equanimity produces a radiance and warmth of being."* The concept embraces the ability to see the bigger picture, and also "refers to balance, to remaining centered in the middle of whatever is happening."

They identify seven mental qualities which can support the development of equanimity (Box 5). The many practices involved in MBLE contribute towards these seven qualities, and Equanimity can thus be introduced both in its own right and in relation to other aspects of the course. The core verse used in the Equanimity Meditation is:

May I be free from preference and prejudice.
May I know things just as they are.
May I experience the world knowing me just as I am.
May I see into whatever arises.[24]

My experience with the MBLE course is that people readily accept the notion of being free from prejudice, but question the idea of being free from preference. Some of the concepts above - calmness, balance, all beings having rights, challenging reactive tendencies - can help here.

---

[24] Taken from Ken McLeod's website Unfettered Mind: Pragmatic Buddhism at http://www. unfetteredmind.org/four-immeasurables (accessed 10 December 2012).

1. Integrity. When we live and act with integrity or virtue, we feel confident about our actions and words, which results in the equanimity of blamelessness.

2. Faith. While any kind of faith can provide equanimity, faith grounded in wisdom is especially powerful.

3. A well-developed mind. Much as we might develop physical strength, balance, and stability of the body in a gym, so too can we develop strength, balance and stability of the mind. This is done through practices that cultivate calm, concentration and mindfulness.

4. Well-being. We do not need to leave well-being to chance. We often overlook the well-being that is easily available in daily life – such as taking time to enjoy one's tea or the sunset.

5. Understanding or wisdom. Wisdom is an important factor in learning to have an accepting awareness, to be present for whatever is happening without the mind or heart contracting or resisting. Wisdom can teach us to separate people's actions from who they are. We can agree or disagree with their actions, but remain balanced in our relationship with them.

6. Insight, a deep seeing into the nature of things as they are. One of the primary insights is the nature of impermanence. In the deepest forms of this insight, we see that things change so quickly that we can't hold onto anything, and eventually the mind lets go of clinging. Letting go brings equanimity; the greater the letting go, the deeper the equanimity.

7. Freedom, which comes as we begin to let go of our reactive tendencies. We can get a taste of what this means by noticing areas in which we were once reactive but are no longer.

Source; Fronsdal and Pandita (2005) See also http://www.insightmeditationcenter.org/books-articles/articles/equanimity/ (accessed 10 December 2012)

AN INTEGRATED APPROACH TO THE FOUR IMMEASURABLES

In recent years a number of writers have developed and enriched understanding of some or all of the Four Immeasurables. Salzberg (1995) focuses on Loving-Kindness, incorporating her discussion of the other three within this. Gilbert gives primacy to compassion. He argues that "Within Buddhism, 'compassion' and 'kindness' have different meanings" (2010a:6-7), and then gives metta, mudita, karuna and upekkha as examples. Wallace, McLeod, and Nyaponika Thera take an integrated approach, seeing the Four Immeasurables as a "pattern that connects" (Bateson 1973:10). They outline ways in which each quality can support the others, relating in particular to the treatment of the Near and Far Enemies.

The Brahma-Viharas appear frequently in the Nikāyas, usually involving a standard formula referring to the cultivation of the qualities, enabling one to "dwell thus, equanimous, mindful and clearly aware"[25]. This occurs at least twelve times in Majjhima Nikāya, five times in Dīgha Nikāya, and once each in Samyutta Nikāya and Anguttara Nikāya. In several suttas the advice moves beyond the standard formula to indicate further the value of the qualities. Thus, 'The Greater Discourse of Advice to Rāhula' sees meditation on the four as leading to the abandonment of ill will, cruelty, discontent and aversion.

Loving-Kindness is considered in its own right in nine suttas in Majjhima Nikāya, and six times in Anguttara Nikāya. Compassion and Empathetic-Joy[26] are rarely considered separately, while Equanimity is frequently discussed in other contexts, in particular as one of the Seven Factors of Enlightenment. This separate discussion occurs at least eleven times in Majjhima Nikāya, twice in Samyutta Nikāya, and six times in Anguttara Nikāya. Equanimity is seen as contributing to the purification of mindfulness, while in The Refinement of the Mind II it is argued that the trainee "should from time to time give

---

[25] Samyutta Nikāya 59.

[26] I have chosen this term rather than the alternatives of Sympathetic or Altruistic Joy, and the verb 'rejoicing' suggested by Chodron.

attention to concentration, … to energetic effort, … to equanimity"[27] all three are important.

From the above we may reasonably conclude the following:

1. The Brahma-Viharas have an important role in Buddhist psychology and practice.
2. They are seen as an integrated whole, an Indra's Net.
3. Loving-Kindness has a degree of autonomy, in that it is the only one frequently considered in its own right.
4. Equanimity is a linking quality with several other aspects of Buddhist psychology, in particular with the seven factors of enlightenment.

These considerations lead to Figure 3-2 as a framework for considering the Brahma-Viharas, with Loving-Kindness leading to Compassion and Empathetic Joy, while Equanimity supports all three and in turn interlinks them with the Seven Factors. In part this echoes the comments of Sangharakshita that Compassion is "Love's response to the sufferings of others" and Joy "its reaction to their joys" (1993:182).

After the Nikayas, the next important treatment of the Brahma-Viharas is in Chapter IX of Buddhaghosa's Visuddhimagga. Three aspects of his extensive analysis (Table 3.6) are particularly relevant here. The first is his practical guidance for Brahma-Vihara practice, involving multiple stages beginning with oneself and then extending in a number of directions. This guidance has been adopted by contemporary writers, although the number of directions varies. The second is his detailed explanation of each quality, including the Near and Far Enemies. This analysis has been usefully summarised in tabular form by Fronsdal and Pandita, extended here to include the writings of Wallace and McLeod (Table 3.7).

---

[27] Anguttara Nikāya 35.

Third, Buddhaghosa comments on the relationship between the four qualities and their order: first to promote welfare through loving-kindness, second, to promote the removal of suffering through compassion, third to practice gladness through empathetic joy, and fourth to promote neutrality through equanimity. This lends further support to the characterization given here.

In total we can identify 22 such interrelationships in the contributions of these authors, with all twelve possible connections appear at least once (see Figures 3-3 to 3-5). This reinforces Nyaponika Thera's argument (2008:13) that "Isolated virtues, if unsupported by other qualities which give them either the needed firmness or pliancy, often deteriorate into their own characteristic defects." In the diagrams Equanimity appears as the base, echoing Richmond's (2004) comments: *"With friendliness, compassion and even sympathetic joy, there is always a tendency to apply these feelings just to some people those we like, or those for whom we have sympathy, such as the poor or the oppressed. ... It is only in Equanimity that we are able to turn our compassion impartially to everyone and everything"* (ibid:144).

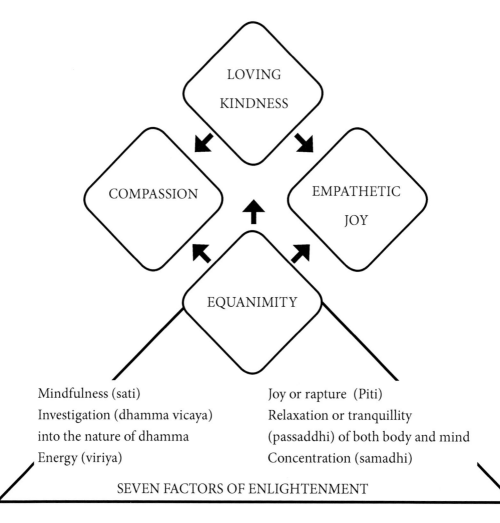

Figure 3-2: THE BRAHMA-VIHARAS

Table 3.6: BRAHMA VIHARAS AS ANALYSED BY BUDDHAGHOSA

	Characteristic	Function	Manifestation	Proximate Cause	Succeeds when it	Fails when it
Mettā Loving-kindness	Promoting welfare	To prefer welfare	Removal of annoyance	Seeing the loveability of beings	Makes ill-will subside	Produces sentimentality
Karunā Compassion	Promoting the alaying of suffering	Not bearing the suffering of others	Non-cruelty	Seeing helplessness in those overwhelmed by suffering	Makes cruelty subside	Produces sorrow
Muditā Empathetic Joy	Gladdening (produced by the success of others)	Being un-envious	Elimination of aversion	Seeing the success of beings	Makes aversion subside	Produces amusement
Upekkhā Equanimity	Promoting objectivity towards beings	To see equality in beings	The subsiding of acquisitiveness and resistance	Seeing ownership of deeds	Makes acquisitiveness and resistance subside	Produces mundane equanimity of the uninformed

Developed from chart by Fronsdal and Pandita (2005)

Table 3.7: BRAHMA VIHARAS AS ANALYSED BY LATER COMMENTATORS

	The Way to Purity	Defining Feature	Things as they are	Near Enemy	Far Enemy
Mettā Loving-kindness	For one who has much ill-will	Intention of good will; the wish for the welfare and happiness of all beings.	Appreciates	Attachment, greed	Hatred, ill will
Karunā Compassion	For one who has much cruelty	Wish to alleviate suffering	Accepts	Pity, grief	Cruelty
Muditā Empathetic Joy	For one who has much aversion	Rejoicing in the success of others; appreciation,	Enjoys	Joy tinged with insincerity or personal identification; forms of joy that are excessive such as elation, exuberance	Envy, jealousy, aversion
Upekkhā Equanimity	For one who has much attachment	Seeing equality in beings, balanced, non-reactive, non-partial, awareness; quieting of resentment and approval	Sees	Indifference, foolish unknowing	Greed, taking of sides, partiality, resentment, reactivity

Developed from chart by Fronsdal and Pandita (2005)

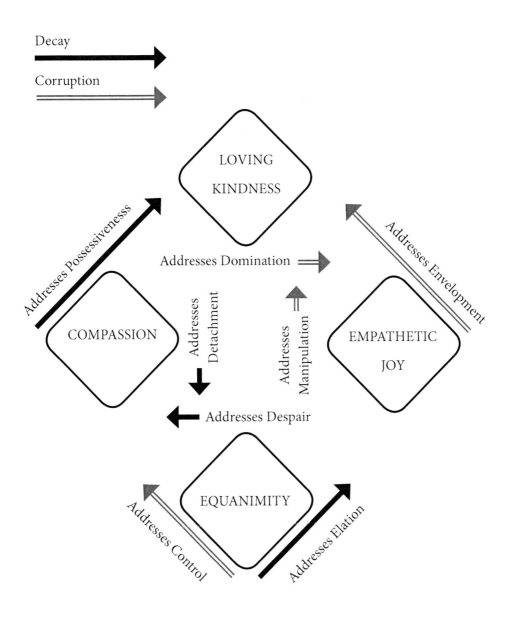

Decay

Corruption

LOVING KINDNESS

Addresses Possessivenesss

Addresses Domination

Addresses Envelopment

COMPASSION

Addresses Detachment

Addresses Manipulation

EMPATHETIC JOY

Addresses Despair

EQUANIMITY

Addresses Control

Addresses Elation

Figure 3-3: SUPPORT RELATIONSHIPS BETWEEN THE FOUR IMMEASURABLES

Text from McLeod (2001)

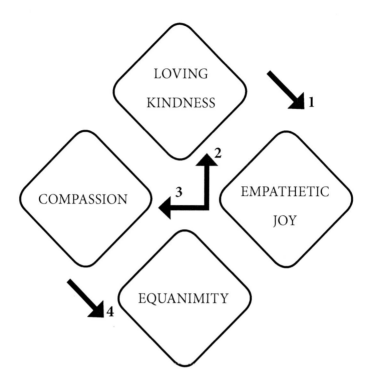

Figure 3-4: SUPPORT RELATIONSHIPS BETWEEN THE FOUR IMMEASURABLES

Text from Wallace (2004)

1 Loving kindness can become about self-centred attachment – about me and mine - Equanimity helps recognise it is about all.

2 Empathetic Joy can fall into frivolity and hedonism –focussing on the fruits of happiness, life is just to be happy – Loving kindness is yearning may we find genuine happiness - and the causes of this.

3 Compassion can become sadness and grief – Altruistic joy helps recognise that it is not all suffering – attending to the joys and virtues of others and ourselves.

4 Equanimity can become aloof indifference – I give up, I don't care anymore – Compassion attends to the suffering in the world.

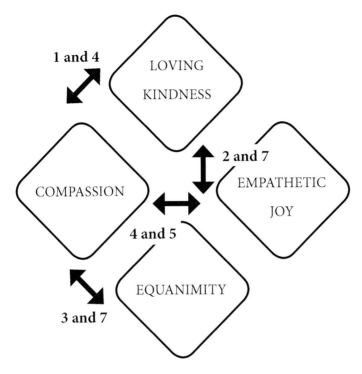

Figure 3-5: SUPPORT RELATIONSHIPS BETWEEN THE FOUR IMMEASURABLES

Text from Nyanaponika Thera (1994)

1 Unbounded love guards compassion against turning into partiality, prevents it from making discriminations by selecting and excluding and thus protects it from falling into partiality or aversion against the excluded side.

2 Love imparts to equanimity its selflessness, its boundless nature and even its fervour. For fervour, too, transformed and controlled, is part of perfect equanimity, strengthening its power of keen penetration and wise restraint.

3 Compassion guards equanimity from falling into a cold indifference, and keeps it from indolent or selfish isolation.

4 Compassion prevents love and sympathetic joy from forgetting that, while both are enjoying or giving temporary and limited happiness, there still exist at that time most dreadful states of suffering in the world.

5 Empathetic joy holds compassion back from becoming overwhelmed by the sight of the world's suffering, from being absorbed by it to the exclusion of everything else.

6 Empathetic joy gives to equanimity the mild serenity that softens its stern appearance; a smile that gives solace and hope, fearlessness and confidence: "Wide open are the doors to deliverance," thus it speaks.

7 Equanimity rooted in insight is the guiding and restraining power for the other three sublime states. It points out to them the direction they have to take, and sees to it that this direction is followed. Equanimity guards love and compassion from being dissipated in vain quests and from going astray in the labyrinths of uncontrolled emotion. Equanimity, being a vigilant self-control for the sake of the final goal, does not allow empathetic joy to rest content with humble results, forgetting the real aims we have to strive for.

Earlier in this chapter we explored the case for including the Four Immeasurables explicitly in a mindfulness course, and the way they can support each other. We can now extend that argument by showing the ways in which each quality helps address the Near Enemies of the other qualities, as shown in Table 3.8.

Table 3.8: SUPPORTING LINKS BETWEEN THE FOUR IMMEASURABLES	
Loving Kindness	Far Enemies: Hatred, ill will, anger Near Enemies: Attachment, greed, conditional love
Compassion	Compassion prevents loving-kindness from forgetting that, while both are enjoying or giving temporary and limited happiness, there still exists much suffering in the world.
Empathetic Joy	Empathetic Joy brings a sense of power, setting boundaries externally and internally.
Equanimity	Equanimity guards love from being dissipated and from going astray in uncontrolled emotion. It helps us recognise that our concerns and interests are with all living beings, challenging any tendency to self-centred attachment.

Compassion	Far Enemies: Cruelty Near Enemies: Pity, grief
Loving Kindness	Loving-kindness guards against partiality, prevents compassion from discrimination by selecting and excluding and thus protects it from falling into partiality or aversion against the excluded side.
Empathetic Joy	Empathetic Joy helps to recognise that it is not all suffering and grief, and that we can attend also to the joys and virtues of ourselves and others; it holds compassion back from becoming overwhelmed by the sight of the world's suffering, from being absorbed by it to the exclusion of everything else.
Equanimity	Equanimity guards compassion from being dissipated and from going astray in uncontrolled emotion. It helps develop composure and internal calm allowing one to know what can or cannot be done.

Empathetic Joy	Far Enemies: Envy, jealousy, aversion Near Enemies: Joy tinged with insincerity or personal identification; forms of joy that are excessive such as elation, exuberance; hedonism
Loving Kindness	Loving-kindness brings us back to the desire that all beings will find genuine happiness and its causes, avoiding frivolity and hedonism.
Compassion	Compassion prevents empathetic joy from forgetting that, while both are enjoying or giving temporary and limited happiness, there still exists much suffering in the world. Empathetic joy needs understanding and compassion and equanimity if you are to avoid becoming a Pollyanna.
Equanimity	Equanimity addresses elation by bringing attention to the tendency to react to whatever arises in experience; being a vigilant self-control for the sake of the final goal, does not allow sympathetic joy to rest content with humble results, forgetting the real aims we have to strive for.

Equanimity	Far Enemies: Greed, resentment, partiality Near Enemies: Indifference, foolish unknowing
Loving Kindness	Loving-kindness addresses indifference and detachment, which is a form of shutting down. It imparts to equanimity its selflessness, its boundless nature and even its fervour. For fervour, too, transformed and controlled, is part of perfect equanimity, strengthening its power of keen penetration and wise restraint.
Compassion	Compassion attends to and reminds us of the suffering in the world; it guards equanimity from falling into a cold indifference, and keeps it from indolent or selfish isolation.

Empathetic Joy	Empathetic joy gives to equanimity the mild serenity that softens its stern appearance. It is the smile that persists in spite of our knowledge of the world's suffering, a smile that gives solace and hope, fearlessness and confidence.

Some of these connections are also to be found in the literature on compassion. Thus Neff (2011) defines self-compassion as having three core components: self-kindness, recognition of our common humanity, and mindfulness. The first of these, of course, links strongly to loving-kindness, the second, less obviously, to equanimity. She writes: *"Although a sense of belongingness can be found within group identities, it is still limited. As long as we're identifying with subsets of people rather than the entire human race, we're creating divisions that separate us from our fellows. Sadly, these divisions often lead to prejudice and hatred"* (2011:67). But on a more positive note *"psychologists have discovered that when our sense of belonging extends to the whole human community rather than stopping at the boundaries of our own social groups, conflict is dramatically lessened"* (ibid:68).

Recognition of the value, and interconnection, of these qualities is extending into clinical psychology. A special issue of the Journal of Clinical Psychology: In Session considers what it calls the "Sisters of Mindfulness" – forgiveness, gratitude, loving-kindness, compassion, acceptance and best-self visualisation – and comments: *"The sisters of mindfulness described in this issue are a Westernized extension of the Buddhist conception, the Brahmaviharas or "The Four Immeasurables". ... It seems that these concepts are inextricable and interdependent. To practice mindfulness, we must approach ourselves with great gentleness and generosity of spirit, exactly the type of qualities that the sister skills embody"* (Rosenzweig 2013: 794,796).

- Wishing others well, including those people you get on with and those who are more of a challenge; being happy for others when they achieve something and sharing in their happiness.

- Loving kindness - I take more time with people, have more patience with them, more readily accept that they are well intentioned. Compassion - I think I probably have always felt compassion, but perhaps see it in a broader sense now. Joy - again, I feel that I do take genuine pleasure in others success, perhaps I am learning to enjoy my own achievements more and berate myself less. Equanimity - the one that I think the course has helped me most with. In some cases more detachment, some cases more attachment but I am definitely (in my own humble opinion) getting a better balance in my head.

- I struggle with these at times as I can get irritable with others but I do try and am succeeding more in having compassion for others. Joy and equanimity are things I already had, and feel I am developing more. Loving kindness is also something I am developing more.

- I think all of them have impacted most on my two main relationships - with mother and partner. I'm a full time carer for my mother who has advanced Alzheimer's disease. This, together with the loss of work/status/job satisfaction that resulted, and the frustrations of trying to manage the inadequate care system, has been stressful and challenging, and meditating on all of the four immeasurables has helped me to cope better and be more positive.

- This is really important for me in dealing with being judgemental, trying to be impartial and trying to be less reactive. Even when I don't succeed, at least I'm aware of these tendencies and can continue to work on them.

- I try and take the "moral high ground" where I can and look for the best in people - I think I'm more aware of trying to do that consciously now.

4. POSITIVE PSYCHOLOGY

In this chapter we look at positive psychology, and explain why six themes related to this are included in Mindfulness Based Life Enhancement. These are Gratitude, Hope, Optimism, Forgiveness, Addressing Negativity and Savouring. These are explained here, with the emphasis on the way each links to and contributes to the overall objectives of MBLE, and the other aspects of it, in particular mindfulness and the Four Immeasurables.

In 1998 the President of the American Psychological Association, Martin Seligman, argued that psychology needed to move beyond its focus on mental illness to understand positive emotion and the pursuit of happiness. With Csikszentmihalyi he argued that the discipline had been dominated by a focus on pathology to the neglect of the positive features that make life worth living (2000).

Since then there has been growing interest in positive psychology, and many books provide practical guidance on introducing its findings into everyday life. The range of themes is extensive; Seligman and Peterson (in Seligman 2003: 134-161) identify 24 personal strengths under six headings (Table 4.1). A number of these are addressed by mindfulness, mindful learning and the Four Immeasurables, and it would be inappropriate to seek to encompass them all directly - this would make it a course in positive psychology rather than mindfulness. But after taking advice from a colleague with expertise in this field, I incorporated into Mindfulness Based Life Enhancement six themes, four of which appear explicitly in Table 4.1.

Table 4.1: PERSONAL STRENGTHS AND VIRTUES		
STRENGTHS OF WISDOM AND KNOWLEDGE	**STRENGTHS OF COURAGE**	**STRENGTHS OF TRANSCENDENCE**
Creativity (originality, ingenuity)	Bravery (valour)	Appreciation of beauty and excellence (awe, wonder, elevation)
Curiosity (interest, novelty-seeking, openness to experience)	Persistence (perseverance, industriousness)	Gratitude
Open-mindedness (judgment, critical thinking).	Integrity (authenticity, honesty)	Hope (optimism, future-mindedness, future orientation)
Love of learning	Vitality (zest, enthusiasm, vigour, energy)	Humour (playfulness)
Perspective (wisdom)		Spirituality (religiousness, faith, purpose)

STRENGTHS OF HUMANITY	**STRENGTHS OF JUSTICE**	**STRENGTHS OF TEMPERANCE**
Love	Citizenship (social responsibility, loyalty, teamwork)	Forgiveness and mercy
Kindness (generosity, nurturance, care, compassion, altruistic love, "niceness")	Fairness	Humility / Modesty
Social intelligence (emotional intelligence, personal intelligence)	Leadership	Prudence
		Self-regulation (self-control)

Seligman has subsequently developed his thinking to argue that authentic happiness theory is one-dimensional, and that well-being theory is broader in scope, addressing five elements:

- Positive emotion
- Engagement
- Relationships
- Meaning
- Achievement.

The 24 strengths identified in Table 4.1 *"underpin all five elements, not just engagement: deploying your highest strengths leads to more positive emotion, to more meaning, to more accomplishment, and to better relationships"* (2011:24). All five elements are addressed in Mindfulness Based Life Enhancement, although the fifth – achievement - is implicit; we return to this later.

Seligman links these to Huppert and So's (2009) measurement of flourishing, for which "an individual must have all the 'core features' below and three of the six 'additional features'

- Core features: Positive emotions, engagement and interest, meaning and purpose
- Additional features: Self-esteem, optimism, resilience, vitality, self-determination, and positive relationships (ibid:26-7).

Again, these are all addressed in Mindfulness Based Life Enhancement, with the exception that self-compassion is addressed, rather than self-esteem, here endorsing the comment of Neff, who argues that *"unlike self-esteem, the good feelings of self-compassion do not depend on being special and above average, or on meeting ideal goals. ... The bottom line is that according to the science, self-compassion appears to offer the same advantages as high self-esteem, with no discernible downsides"* (2011:153).

ADDRESSING NEGATIVITY

Here we consider several related themes which address the balance between the positive and negative, including the negativity bias, the 40% solution, the Broaden-and-Build theory of positive emotions, disputing negativity, and cognitive distortions.

NEGATIVITY BIAS[28]

Addressing the negative is an important theme in MBSR; thus in McCown et al's (2010) summary of weekly themes, the first week is concerned with the argument that "There's more right than wrong with you", while week four focuses on the "Shadow of Stress (Unpleasant Events)". In MBLE this theme is raised at the outset, identifying the negativity bias - the psychological phenomenon by which we pay more attention to and give more weight to negative rather than positive experiences or other kinds of information. Examples include the following:

- When given a piece of positive information and a piece of negative information about a stranger, people's judgment of the stranger will be negative, rather than neutral (assuming the two pieces of information are not severely imbalanced).
- If a person has a good experience and a bad experience close together, they will feel worse than neutral. This is true even if they would independently judge the two experiences to be of similar magnitude.
- Negative information in the simple form of negation has greater impact and creates more attention than similar positive information in the form of affirmation. For example, describing a behaviour in an affirmation elicits less attention and cognitive processing than describing the same behaviour using a negation. This is related to information processing on negation in cognitive psychology.
- Very often negativity bias is confused with loss aversion.

---

[28]http://psychology.wikia.com/wiki/Negativity_bias'

- When put in an environment with a variety of information to pay attention to, people will immediately notice the threats instead of the opportunities or the signals of safety.

Baumeister et al (2001:355) provide a number of illustrations of the negativity bias. *"In everyday life, bad events have stronger and more lasting consequences than comparable good events. Close relationships are more deeply and conclusively affected by destructive actions than by constructive ones, by negative communications than positive ones, and by conflict than harmony. Even outside of close relationships, unfriendly or conflictual interactions are seen as stronger and have bigger effects than friendly, harmonious ones. Bad moods and negative emotions have stronger effects than good ones on cognitive processing. ... The preponderance of words for bad emotions, contrasted with the greater frequency of good emotions, suggests that bad emotions have more power. Some patterns of learning suggest that bad things are more quickly and effectively learned than corresponding good things."* They argue that research has repeatedly shown that we give more attention to bad things than good, we are more motivated to avoid the bad than to embrace the good, we are more strongly affected by bad feedback rather than good, and bad health has a greater impact on happiness than good health.

They also briefly consider the practical implications by exploring happiness. *"We have concluded that bad is stronger than good, yet a wealth of data suggest that life is good and people are largely happy (D. G. Myers. 1992). How can good overcome the greater power of bad to make life seemingly so wonderful? There are several answers. Good can overcome bad by force of numbers. To maximize the power of good, these numbers must be increased. This can be done by creating more goods. For example, in a romantic relationship each partner can make an effort to be nice to the other consistently. Such small acts of kindness are important for combating the bads that will typically occur. Indeed, if Gottnan (1994) is correct, the ratio should be at least five goods for every bad. Likewise, individuals can make an effort to recognize and appreciate the goods that they have celebrating each small success, being thankful for health, and having gratitude for supportive others"* (ibid:361).

There are two valuable counter-themes to the negativity bias. The first is proposed by Lyubomirsky (2007): while half of happiness is "set" by genetics and 10% by "circumstances," there is a full 40% subject to our constructive, creative, intentional activity. *"Thus the key to happiness lies NOT in changing our genetic makeup (which is impossible) and not in changing our circumstances (i.e., seeking wealth or attraction or better colleagues, which is usually impractical), but in our daily intentional activities... what we do in our daily lives and how we think."* (ibid:22) She has identified multiple examples of the behaviour patterns of very happy people to illustrate this (Table 4.2).

Table 4.2: THE THINKING AND BEHAVIOUR PATTERNS OF THE HAPPIEST
• They devote a great amount of time to their family and friends, nurturing and enjoying those relationships.
• They are comfortable expressing gratitude for all they have.
• They are often the first to offer a helping hand to co-workers and passers-by.
• They practise optimism when imagining their futures.
• They savour life's pleasures and try to live in the present moment.
• They make physical exercise a weekly and sometimes daily habit.
• They are deeply committed to life-long goals and ambitions (e.g., fighting fraud, building cabinets, or teaching their children their deeply held values).
• And, last but not least, the happiest people do have their share of stresses, crises and even tragedies. They may become just as distressed and emotional in such circumstances as you or I, but their secret weapon is the poise and strength they show in coping in the face of challenge.
Lyubomirsky 2007:23

THE BROADEN-AND-BUILD THEORY OF POSITIVE EMOTIONS[29]

The second theme relating to the balance between positive and negative is Fredrickson's Broaden-and-Build Theory of Positive Emotions (2009). She identifies four key areas:

- Intellectual resources, which involves developing problem solving skills and learning new information
- Physical resources, which involve developing coordination, strength and cardiovascular health
- Social resources, which involve solidifying existing bonds and making new ones
- Psychological resources, which involve developing resilience and optimis, and a sense of identity and goal orientation.

Fredrickson argues that while negative emotions narrow people's ideas about possible actions, positive emotions do the exact opposite. First, they Broaden ideas, bringing a more open awareness of thoughts and actions, allowing us to be more receptive and creative. Second, this expansive awareness allows us to build and discover new skills, new knowledge, and new ways of being.

DISPUTING NEGATIVITY

Returning to Negativity, several cognitive approaches have been suggested. Originally developed by Albert Ellis, creator of Rational Emotive Behavioural Therapy, the ABCDE model is intended to help challenge negative thinking and thinking errors. Ellis summarised his approach thus: "REBT is based on the assumption that what we label our 'emotional' reactions are largely caused by our conscious and unconscious evaluations, interpretations and philosophies. Thus we feel anxious or depressed because we strongly convince ourselves that it is terrible when we fail at something or that we can't stand the pain of being rejected."[30]

---

[29] For more on this theory see http://www.unc.edu/peplab/broaden_build.html

[30] http://www.rebt.ws/REBT%20explained.html

To challenge these assumptions, we start with ABC:

- **A for Action** is the event, situation, sensation, memory or image that starts off the chain of thoughts and feelings
- **B for Belief** is the thought or attitude that causes us to see the event in a certain way (see the Cognitive Distortions below)
- **C for Consequence** is the reaction of emotion (e.g.: Depression, guilt, hurt, anger, shame, jealousy, envy, anxiety) and behaviour (e.g. avoidance, withdrawing, escape, using alcohol, seeking reassurance, procrastination) that follows in response to the original event seen in this way.

We often assume that A provokes C and that we are therefore powerless to stop C. REBT challenges this assumption and insists that the emotional response comes from the thought, not from the event, that one's emotion and behaviour come from one's chosen belief system and not from the other person's action. The other person's action may stimulate our beliefs into reacting, but without those beliefs we would react quite differently.

To challenge these assumptions, we go to DE:

- **D for Dispute** (that is, question and examine) **B:** contest the beliefs and generate alternatives
- **E for Effect or Energisation** of alternative thoughts and beliefs **(D):** observe the energisation that occurs as you succeed in dealing with negative beliefs

---

Box 6: AN EXAMPLE OF ABCDE

A   A friend passes you in the street without speaking to you

B   You believe that she is ignoring you because she doesn't like you, and since it is important to you that people like you, you conclude she is telling you, by ignoring you, that you do not count

C   Your emotional reaction is one of anger and depression, and your behaviour is then to avoid the 'former' friend

D   You take the view instead that your friend had something on her mind, and therefore didn't notice you; she continues to be a friend and you will help if you can

E   Your emotional reaction is now one of concern, and your behaviour is to make contact with the friend.

COGNITIVE DISTORTIONS

Cognitive distortions are inaccurate thoughts which reinforce negative thinking or emotions - telling ourselves things that sound rational and accurate, but really only serve to keep us feeling bad about ourselves. If we become more mindful of these, we can gradually learn to recognise their arising, and weaken their impact.

Beck (1976) first proposed the theory behind cognitive distortions and Burns (1980) popularised it with common names and examples for the distortions[31], which include all-or-nothing thinking, overgeneralisation and catastrophising. It is worth adding that lists of 'cognitive biases and distortions' found in the texts on CBT find a close parallel with similar discussions in the organisational strategy literature, where the concern is to help strategists avoid fixed and narrow patterns of interpretation and behaviour which can have devastating consequences for their organisation.

LEARNING TO ARGUE WITH YOURSELF

Seligman (2003:95-7) argues that there are four important ways to make your disputations convincing:

- Evidence: show to yourself that the negative belief is factually incorrect. This is not 'positive thinking', the use of upbeat statements such as "Every day, in every way, I'm getting better and better" in the absence of evidence, or even in the face of contrary evidence. It is about accuracy.
- Alternatives: scan for all possible contributing causes, generating alternative beliefs, alternative possibilities.
- Implications: this involves decatastrophizing. Even if the belief is true, you say to yourself, what are its implications? What is the worst-case scenario?

---

[31] Listings of these are available on many websites. See for example http://en.wikipedia.org/wiki/Cognitive_distortion and http://www.psychologytoday.com/blog/in-practice/201301/50-common-cognitive-distortions

- Usefulness: Sometimes the consequences of holding a belief matter more than its truth. Is the belief destructive? What good will it do me to dwell on the belief that the world should be fair? Another tactic is to detail all the ways you can change the situation in the future. Even if the belief is true now, is the situation changeable? How can you go about changing it?

OPTIMISM

Seligman contrasts optimists and pessimists. The latter "tend to believe bad events will last a long time, will undermine everything they do, and are their own fault." By contrast optimists, faced with the same circumstances, "tend to believe defeat is just a temporary setback, that its causes are confined to this one case" (2006:5). He continues: *"These two habits of thinking about causes have consequences. Literally hundreds of studies show that pessimists give up more easily and get depressed more often. These experiments also show that optimists do much better in school and college, at work and on the playing field. They regularly exceed the predictions of aptitude tests. When optimists run for office, they are more apt to be elected than pessimists are. Their health is unusually good. They age well, much freer than most of us from the usual physical ills of middle age. Evidence suggests they may even live longer."* (ibid.)

In the Buddhist literature optimism has been linked to change - the potential for transformation. Ricard comments: *"There is an even deeper dimension to optimism, that of realizing the potential for transformation that is in every human being, regardless of his or her condition. It is that potential, in the end, that gives meaning to human life. The ultimate pessimism is in thinking that life in general is not worth living. The ultimate optimism lies in understanding that every passing moment is a treasure, in joy as in adversity. These are not subtle nuances, but a fundamental difference in the way of seeing things. This divergence of perspective depends on whether or not we have found within ourselves the fulfilment that alone fuels inner peace"* (2007:225). He provides a thought experiment, contrasting optimistic and pessimistic views of an airplane voyage, which MBLE participants are encouraged to try, as a way to *"appreciate the difference between these two states of mind and understand how they came about simply through the workings of your mind although the outer situation remained the same"* (ibid:226).

HOPE

Ricard is again helpful when we consider hope, *"the conviction that one can find the means to attain one's goals and develop the motivation necessary to do so"* (2007:220). He argues that hope can improve students' test results and athletes' performance; it can make illness more bearable, and pain itself (from burns, arthritis, spinal injuries, or blindness, for example) easier to tolerate.

Frederickson contrasts hope with other aspects of positivity, arguing that it becomes important in adverse circumstances. *"Hope arises precisely within those moments when hopelessness or despair seem just as likely. … Deep within the core of hope is the belief that things can change. … It motivates you to tap into your own capabilities and inventiveness to turn things around. It inspires you to plan for a better future"* (2009:43).

For Boyatzis and McKee (2005) hope is one of the three elements of resonant leadership, along with mindfulness and compassion. McKee, Johnston and Massimilian (2006)[32] argue that hope positively impacts on our brains and hormones, allowing us to feel calm, happy, amused and optimistic. We are up for the challenges ahead. They see hope as contagious, and have drawn three lessons for leaders:

- They need to have dreams and aspirations, but also to be in touch with the people who surround them. This helps to form a desired image of the future that can be shared.
- They need to be optimistic and believe in their ability to effect change.
- They must see the desired future as realistic.

---

[32] http://www.iveybusinessjournal.com/topics/leadership/mindfulness-hope-and-compassion-a-leader%E2%80%99s-road-map-to-renewal

McCullough links hope with both mindfulness and savouring (which we discuss below), arguing that for hopeful people "the very pursuit of goals in itself brings meaning and purpose to their lives, and these pursuits themselves - independent of whether the goals themselves are reached - should be savored rather than simply endured. This propensity to relish the very steps on the road to accomplishing one's goals is a sort of mindfulness that imbues goal pursuits - independent of whether those goals are ever realized - with meaning of their own" (2002:302).

GRATITUDE

McCullough argues that there is a strong correlation in dispositions towards gratitude and hope, and that the characteristic that explains this may be mindful attentiveness: "Grateful and hopeful people may both possess the cognitive habit of savoring their life circumstances, appreciating fully the good circumstances that come their way in the past and the meaningfulness of the goal pursuits they undertake in the present"(2001:3103).

The positive psychology literature includes many examples of the way gratitude helps enhance life (Table 4.3), as well as suggestions of ways to increase a sense of gratitude (Table 4.4).

Table 4.3: HOW GRATITUDE BOOSTS HAPPINESS
1. Grateful thinking promotes the savouring of positive life experiences
2. Expressing gratitude bolsters self-worth and self esteem
3. Gratitude helps people cope with stress and trauma. Expressing gratefulness during personal adversity like loss or chronic illness, as hard as that might be, can help you adjust, move on and perhaps begin anew.
4. The expression of gratitude encourages moral behaviour.
5. Gratitude can help build social bonds, strengthening existing relationships and nurturing new ones.
6. Expressing gratitude tends to inhibit invidious comparisons with others.

7. The practice of gratitude is incompatible with negative emotions and may actually diminish or deter such feelings as anger, bitterness and greed.
8. Gratitude helps us to thwart hedonic adaptation.

Lyubomirsky 2007

Emmons and Stern (2013) provide an overall summary of the value of gratitude, arguing that clinical trials show it can lower blood pressure, improve immune function, promote happiness and well-being, and spur acts of helpfulness, generosity, and cooperation.

Table 4.4: BECOMING MORE GRATEFUL

1. Keep a gratitude journal	5. Use your senses
2. Remember the bad	6. Use visual reminders
3. Ask yourself three questions: what you have received from someone, what you have given to them and what trouble you have caused them.	7. Swear an oath to be more grateful
	8. Think grateful thoughts
	9. Acting grateful is being grateful
4. Pray	10. Be grateful to your enemies

Emmons 2007

There are three gratitude activities which can be practised to enhance mindfulness-based living. The first is to ritualise gratitude, which could involve a journal, or a listing of three things that went well each day. The second is to write a letter to someone who has made a major difference to your life (Seligman 2003), and then read it to them in person. The third is to follow the tradition found in many communities of giving thanks for food before eating it, developing your own practice of doing this. One example has been offered by Thich Nhat Hanh - the Five Contemplations[33].

1. "This food is the gift of the whole universe: the earth, the sky, numerous living beings, and much hard, loving work.

2. May we eat with mindfulness and gratitude so as to be worthy to receive it.

3. May we recognize and transform our unwholesome mental formations, especially our greed, and learn to eat with moderation.

4. May we keep our compassion alive by eating in such a way that we reduce the suffering of living beings, preserve our planet, and reverse the process of global warming.

5. We accept this food so that we may nurture our sisterhood and brotherhood, strengthen our community, and nourish our ideal of serving all living beings."

FORGIVENESS[34]

As we shall see later, forgiveness emerges as perhaps the most difficult aspect of MBLE for many participants, although they recognise its importance. Narayanasamy comments that *"Macaskill (2002) suggests that people who forgive almost always derive positive effects in terms of healing. The issue of forgiveness is closely linked with peace, as the former can bring about the latter. Forgiveness leads to resolution and this can be very comforting"* (2010:47).

While Macaskill considers that forgiveness is not easy to define, *"as a working definition I suggest that achieving a state of forgiving involves giving up feelings of hurt and ill will towards the perpetrator, no longer being pre-occupied with the hurtful event and spending significant amounts of time thinking about it. Forgiveness can be thought to have truly occurred when the individual can*

---

[33] http://www.mindfulnessbell.org/documents/Five_Contemplations.pdf

[34] For this I have relied heavily on the advice of my colleague Ann Macaskill, who supplied much of the material on forgiveness used on the MBLE course. Unless otherwise indicated all quotations in this section are taken from Macaskill 2002.

begin to pick up the threads of their life and start moving forward in a healthy constructive way" (2002:6). There are a number of factors that victims have to consider and make decisions about when coming to a judgment about the perceived severity of wrongdoing against them (Table 4.5).

Table 4.5: JUDGING THE SEVERITY OF WRONGDOING
• The degree of the perceived wrong. Where is this offence on a continuum from massive offence to trivial?
• The amount of distress engendered by the wrongdoing. What is the emotional impact of the transgression? Again this will be on a continuum from major to minor.
• The perceived intentionality of the transgression. It may be judged to be accidental, in which case it will be judged less severely with less direct blame on the perpetrator. The event could be the result of negligence and then there is likely to be some more direct blaming of the perpetrator, with edicts that s/he should be more careful. If it is judged to be intentional, then it will be rated on a scale of severity.
• The quantity of wrongdoing will be assessed. Consideration will be given to the way in which the perpetrator has behaved towards the victim and others in the past. If this appears to be an isolated incident it will tend to be viewed differently than if it were part of a frequently observed pattern of behaviour on the perpetrator's part. Here historical considerations may arise and this factor may be particularly salient when considering perceived wrongdoing that has an inter group aspect to it.
• The nature of the previous relationship the victim had with the perpetrator. Here the salient features are likely to be the closeness of their relationship and its length.
• Some consideration will also be given to whether there are any mitigating circumstances that may help to explain or even partly excuse the perpetrator's behaviour.

It may be that the perpetrator was perceived to be acting out of character or stressed or hitting out because they themselves had been hurt in some way. There are many possibilities under this category. It is frequently the case that there is some delay in considering the area of mitigation of responsibility. Often in the initial stages of shock, anger and hurt, the victim is focussing more on the negative aspects of the perpetrator's behaviour. Consideration of mitigating circumstances usually requires some time to have elapsed since the incident and emotions to be less raw.

- Whether the perpetrator has shown any remorse has been found in research to be influential in determining how easy it is for the victim to begin to forgive the perpetrator. Obviously the more remorseful the perpetrator is the more likely forgiveness is to occur, but it is not a simple relationship and other factors such as the degree of wrongdoing, the amount of hurt and so on, will influence the process significantly.
- Again research has indicated that when perpetrators apologise to victims, forgiveness is more likely to be achieved. This again will however be heavily influenced by the nature of the transgression.

Macaskill 2002

Exploring forgiveness is an important aspect of MBLE, and there are several activities which can help in this. One is to explore wrongdoing - an event where you feel that someone else has wronged you - and consider the difficulty of forgiving, and the costs and benefits of non-forgiveness.

While "The human capacity to forgive is awe-inspiring," (Macaskill 2002:23) it has to be recognised that there are circumstances where "someone feels that forgiveness is not possible for him or her" (Macaskill ibid:23-4). In such cases "There are unfortunately no quick easy solutions. It will take determination and application on the part of victims to work through the anger and hurt and come to some sort of resolution or even forgiveness of what has occurred and professional help can facilitate this" (Macaskill ibid:25-6). But it is important to recognise that "The psychological stress associated with non-forgiveness cannot be over emphasised. The perpetrator caused you hurt in the past and by hanging on to this sense of hurt and grievance with the related feelings of anger and injustice, you are still allowing them to negatively impact on your daily life" (Macaskill ibid:25). An activity that is suggested here is addressing the perpetrator 'in virtual reality'; that is, writing a letter to the perpetrator, but with the proviso that "This is not a letter that you intend to share with the perpetrator or at least not at this stage if ever. … The purpose of writing the letter is:

- to allow you to express exactly what your feelings are at this time about what has happened;
- to tell the perpetrator what it has meant to you;
- to clarify to the perpetrator any ways that you think they have misunderstood or misjudged you;
- perhaps to say what you wish had happened;
- to get everything negative about the situation off your chest."

SAVOURING

Bryant and Veroff (2007) have researched what they term mindful savouring: the things we think and do to intensify or prolong positive feelings. We can savour the past through reminiscence. When they do this, *"people are not necessarily remembering savouring experiences from the past. Rather they are savouring the way they feel when they remember the past"* (2007:198). We can savour the future, through anticipation. And we can savour the present moment.

Bryant and Veroff argue that there are three essential preconditions for savouring. First, you must be relatively free of pressing social and esteem needs. They see mindfulness meditation as an excellent way of doing this: *"Once a person is ready to adopt a savouring orientation, intentional mindfulness techniques can enable the person to let consciousness flow more easily"* (2007:207).

Second, you need to be focused on attending to your present experience. And third, you need to have some degree of awareness of the positive feelings you are identifying, and again they recommend meditation to help achieve this.

Thus practices which enhance mindfulness are precisely those which can help savouring, while enhancing the capacity to savour can increase mindfulness. These are mutually supportive and mutually rewarding processes. Bryant has identified ten strategies which we can use to discover pleasure and satisfaction in everyday moments (Table 4.6).

Table 4.6: SAVOURING: DISCOVERING PLEASURE IN EVERYDAY MOMENTS	
Share positive feelings with others	This involves seeking out others to share the experience with, telling others how much you value the moment.
Build memories	Actively store images for future recall by taking mental photographs, thinking of reminiscing about the event later, either yourself or with others.
Congratulate yourself	Take pride in a hard-won accomplishment. *"It's a fine line between joyous self-congratulation and shameless self-promotion, but don't worry: You'll know if you're crossing it."* (http://www.prevention.com/) The comment of Abbot Christopher Jamison is helpful here: *"People often speak of taking pride in their work. This is fine in so far as it means taking delight in a job well done and enjoying the recognition of others, but it is harmful if it means heightening somebody's sense of self-importance. The danger is that pride transforms self-esteem into self-importance"* (2009:201).

Fine-tune your senses	Intensify pleasure by focusing on certain stimuli in the situation and blocking out others, trying to sharpen your senses through effortful concentration. Shutting out some sensory stimuli while concentrating on others can heighten your enjoyment of positive experiences particularly those that are short-lived. (This is a strategy particularly recommended to participants to try during their Savouring Vacations, enjoying taste, music, the sights of nature etc. see page 100).
Compare downward	Compare the present situation with similar times in the past or with what one imagined the event would be like. Comparing upward makes us feel deprived, but comparing downward can heighten enjoyment. Think about how things could be worse or how things used to be worse. (This strategy requires explicit explanation during the course, as it is easy to think that it involves comparing ourselves with people less fortunate than ourselves, the very antithesis of compassion).
Get absorbed	At times, we savour best when we simply immerse ourselves in the present moment, without deliberate analysis or judgment. This relates closely to Csikszentmihalyi's (1990) concept of flow.
Fake it till you make it	Putting on a happy face - even if you don't feel like it - actually induces greater happiness.
Seize the moment	Some positive events come and go quickly, yet paradoxically reminding ourselves that time is fleeting and joy transitory prompts us to seize positive moments while they last.

Avoid killjoy thinking	Short-circuit negative thoughts that can only dampen enjoyment, such as self-recriminations or worries about others' perceptions. Consciously make the decision to embrace joy.
Say thank-you	Cultivate an "attitude of gratitude." Pinpoint what you're happy about and acknowledge its source. It's not always necessary to outwardly express gratitude, but saying "thank you" to a friend, a stranger, or the universe deepens our happiness by making us more aware of it.
Based on material originally published at Prevention.com[35], and on Bryant and Veroff: Savoring (2007)	

Bryant and Veroff identify four key savouring processes (Table 4.7). The two involving experiential absorption - marvelling and luxuriating - focus on the present, while the other two involve reflection on positive things that have previously occurred. They comment "True wisdom lies in learning to savour in ways that achieve both hedonia and eudaimonia, without trading one form of happiness for the other" (Bryant and Veroff 2007:214).

Table 4.7: THE FOUR MAIN TYPES OF SAVOURING PROCESSES		
	Focus of Attention	
Type of Experience	External World	Internal Self
Cognitive Reflection	Thanksgiving (gratitude)	Basking (pride)
Experiential Absorption	Marvelling (awe)	Luxuriating (physical pleasure)
Source: Bryant and Veroff 2007:137		

---

[35] http://www.prevention.com/

Thanksgiving involves acknowledging or expressing gratitude for blessings, gifts, or favours. An example would be telling others you cherish them. Marvelling involves being struck with awe by an external stimulus, losing sense of self and time – for example, when watching a beautiful sunset, or listening to your favourite music. Basking involves receiving praise or congratulations from self or others. Examples would be awards ceremonies and celebration. Luxuriating involves indulging oneself in pleasurable physical sensations, for example through the mindful enjoyment of a meal.

Bryant and Veroff (2007) propose an activity which they call the Daily Savouring Vacation. Participants in MBLE are encouraged (indeed, instructed!) to do this each day between sessions two and three - and ideally, on a regular basis thereafter.

Table 4.8: SAVOURING: THE DAILY VACATION ACTIVITY
1. Plan and participate in a formal "daily vacation" during which you spend time doing something you find enjoyable for at least 20 minutes. This activity might be going for a walk, sitting quietly in a garden, reading a book, treating yourself to a cup of coffee, going out to eat, visiting a museum or art gallery, taking a shower or soaking in a bathtub, spending time with a friend, or watching a sunset. Be creative in finding sources of enjoyment that you can look forward to and savour. This exercise works best if you seek a variety of experiences in your daily vacations.
2. Before starting each daily vacation, make sure to set aside worries and concerns, pressing responsibilities, and sources of stress for at least 20 minutes, and do your best to structure the situation so as to prevent distractions while you are savouring. Remind yourself not to be judgmental, but rather to see things as if for the first or last time, and to focus on what is happening and what you are feeling as it unfolds in the present.

3. While you are on your daily vacation, try to notice and explicitly acknowledge to yourself each stimulus or sensation that you find pleasurable. Identify your positive feelings and explicitly label them in your mind. Actively build a memory of the feeling and the stimuli associated with it, close your eyes, swish the feeling around in your mind, and outwardly express the positive feeling in some way.

4. At the end of your daily vacation, plan another daily vacation and begin to look forward to it. At the end of the day, look back on your daily vacation, and recall and rekindle the positive feelings you savoured.

5. Make a few notes on your experience.

6. Before our next session, take a few minutes to recall all of your daily vacations. Look back on the activities you enjoyed doing and try to re-experience the positive feelings you felt during each daily vacation. Compare the way you have felt over the past week and the way you feel right now to the way you usually feel during a typical week. People typically report having felt happier a greater percentage of the time during their week of daily vacations and report feeling happier at the end of the week, compared to the way they usually feel.

Bryant and Veroff (2007); Savouring

The comments of MBLE participants (Exhibit 11) show the positive impact of this activity. It relates also to other aspects of the course. Many MBI courses, including MBLE, feature mindful eating of a raisin or some other morsel of food: participants are encouraged to take this further in their informal practice by mindful eating, for example by following the advice of Hanh and Cheung (Table 4.9). And as already mentioned MBLE includes a smiling meditation, which can also be practised informally (Table 4.10).

Exhibit 11: COMMENTS OF PARTICIPANTS: SAVOURING

- The two important ones for me are gratitude and savouring. I do a brief gratitude practice each day and also savouring is becoming very important. I have found that both are brilliant in countering negative thoughts.
- I try to be more mindful and present and enjoy situations generally. When I swim I try to feel the water, breath drawn through arms then legs, making sure joints relax. Enjoy the sensations on skin. Enjoy first cup of tea of the day, then coffee strong and black, savouring bitterness. Mindful of looking at a person when I talk to her/him, really aware and enjoying her/his presence. Really trying to listen and noticing expressions.
- Savour sensation and breath of singing, particularly classical music which asks for emotion and depth. Love the feeling of breath moving through and in body to sustain the sound. Enjoy being me in my body, solid.
- I have become more mindful and more conscious of what is going on in my head. I then try to bring myself back to the moment and concentrate on that and savour more. The former is easier than the latter. I often hear the words from the tape "Where are you now?" echoing in my head!
- I continue to meditate most mornings and try to savour moments in the day. I think I am calmer than before and a little happier.

Table 4.9: SAVOURING: THE SEVEN PRACTICES OF A MINDFUL EATER
1. Honour the food
2. Engage all six senses
3. Serve in modest portions
4. Savour small bites, and chew thoroughly
5. Eat slowly to avoid overeating
6. Don't skip meals
7. Eat a plant-based diet, for your health and for the planet.
Thich Nhat Hanh and Lilian Cheung 2011

Table 4.10: INFORMAL PRACTICE: THE YOGA OF SMILING
1. A smile begins with the eyes. Notice a twinkle, a feeling of amusement in your eyes.
2. Notice how they move naturally as it becomes a smile with the eyes.
3. You should resist smiling with your mouth. It will only grimace, so keep it fixed.
4. When you smile with your eyes, it will spread and your mouth will move naturally and easily into a genuine smile. Let the smile with your mouth come naturally when it is ready.
5. Beam with your eyes, and keep the rest of your face motionless until it breaks into a warm, friendly smile!
http://www.trans4mind.com/personal_development/Vignettes/ SmilingEyes.htm

THE FOUR IMMEASURABLES AND POSITIVE PSYCHOLOGY

There are important links between the Four Immeasurables and Positive Psychology. Several positive psychology researchers have experimented with metta meditation. Fredrickson et al (2008) found that happy people become happier through kindness. They argue that kind people experience more happiness and have happier memories, so kindness, like gratitude, is an important human strength that influences subjective well-being. Cultivating kindness and meditating on loving-kindness are two of the twelve tools to decrease negativity and increase positivity identified by Fredrickson (2009).

Loving-kindness meditation has been explored in positive psychology, and Fredrickson concludes that *"The positivity generated by this form of meditation practice accounts for a wide sweep of benefits in people's lives - from improved abilities to savour and be mindful, to having an easier time accepting themselves, finding positive meaning, and trusting others. Practitioners even suffer fewer aches, pains, colds, and flus. Practising loving-kindness helps people move the riverbed for their day-to-day emotions to higher ground. Ultimately, they become less depressed and more satisfied with life as a whole"* (2009:197).

Oman et al (2008) did research with students showing that meditation reduced stress and increased forgiveness. Johnson et al looked at the effects of loving-kindness meditation with a very different group - individuals suffering from schizophrenia - and concluded: "In light of the limited efficacy of current treatments for negative symptoms, there is a significant need for psychosocial treatments that improve anticipatory pleasure, sociality and motivation" (2009: 5008). Loving-kindness being one, although they recognise that some clients will have difficulty with this, and might benefit more from basic mindfulness exercises.

Lyubomirsky found that doing acts of kindness on a regular basis makes people happy for an extended period. She says that being kind and generous leads you to perceive others more positively and more charitably. And helping others leads people to like you, to appreciate you, to offer gratitude. Lyubomirsky

(2007) includes practising acts of kindness as one of her 12 acts of happiness. Hutcherson et al (2008) found that loving-kindness meditation had significant effects on people's feelings of social connection and positivity toward neutral strangers. Seligman, the founder of positive psychology, reports that spontaneous philanthropic acts can create an "afterglow lasting the whole day" (2003:9). Otake et al found that "kindness is an important human strength that influences subjective well-being" (2006:370.)

On occasion the positive thinking aspect of positive psychology is characterised as "empty-headed, delusional, wishful or Pollyannish" (Aspinwall 2005:754), but as she continues, such characterisations "are at odds with a great deal of evidence suggesting considerable benefits of optimism and positive affect" (ibid). And Fredrickson reinforces this: "Without negativity you become Pollyanna, with a forced clown smile painted on your face" (2009:136).

There is a danger that positive psychology focuses too much on the individual. Metta meditation can easily become something to be practised primarily for its beneficial effects on the meditator: "the positivity generated by this form of meditation practice accounts for a wide sweep of benefits in people's lives" (Fredrickson 2009: 197). But much of the research in the field lends support to the wider perspective being argued here. Thus Lutz and Davidson studied people who have practised compassion meditation for a long period, and concluded that *"the mental expertise to cultivate positive emotion alters the activation of circuitries previously linked to empathy"* (2008:1).

Ricard refers to Seligman's work, but then develops the discussion of "genuine altruism that is motivated by no other reason than to do good for others" (2007:206). The Dalai Lama, in his discussion of the art of happiness, identifies "genuine compassion" as "based on the rationale that all human beings have an innate desire to be happy and overcome suffering just like myself" (1999:92). In both cases, there is an important shift from focus on the individual to focus on all - the domain of the Four Immeasurables, with their emphasis on benefits to others. The benefits to oneself are not primary.

An additional difference is in the sources of happiness. Positive Psychology on occasion focuses on the external, whereas the Four Immeasurables relate to the internal, in particular Sukha, as described by Ricard: "Sukha is the state of lasting well-being that manifests itself when we have freed ourselves of mental blindness and afflictive emotions. It is also the wisdom that allows us to see the world as it is, without veils or distortions. It is, finally, the joy of moving toward inner freedom and the loving-kindness that radiates toward others" (2007:25).

POSITIVE PSYCHOLOGY AND MBLE: A COMPARISON

As we have seen, in Mindfulness Based Life Enhancement the focus from Positive Psychology is on savouring, optimism, hope, gratitude and forgiveness, alongside the challenge to negativity. Several authors have brought together a more comprehensive set of activities, and two such sets are given in Table 4.11 the first from Lyubomirsky (2007), and the second from Fredrickson (2009). These sets of activities are linked to the themes explored and practised in MBLE.

Table 4.11: LINKS BETWEEN POSITIVE PSYCHOLOGY AND MBLE		
Happiness Activities: Lyubomirsky (2007)	Toolkit for Positivity: Fredrickson (2009)	Mindfulness Based Life Enhancement
	Be Open	Mindfulness
Expressing gratitude	Ritualise gratitude	Gratitude
Cultivating optimism		Optimism
Avoiding overthinking and social comparison	Dispute negative thinking	Challenging negative thinking
Practising acts of kindness	Cultivate kindness	Loving kindness
Nurturing social relationships	Create High-quality connections	Four Immeasurables; Dialogue
	Meditate on loving-kindness	Loving kindness

Developing strategies for coping		Challenging negative thinking
Learning to forgive		Forgiveness
Increasing 'flow' experiences		Personal strengths
Savouring life's joys	Savour positivity	Savouring
Committing to your goals	Visualise your future	Personal strengths
Practising religion and spirituality	Meditate mindfully	Mindfulness
Taking care of your body		Mindful Movement
	Develop distractions	Savouring
	Find nearby nature	Mindful walking
	Learn and apply your strengths	Personal strengths

Both authors stress the value of meditation, thus showing once more the mutually supporting links between positive psychology and mindfulness. Thus Lyubomirsky comments on the value of meditation: *"I honestly was surprised to learn how many controlled laboratory and field investigations have been conducted to explore the consequences of the practice of meditation. An avalanche of studies have shown that meditation has multiple positive effects on a person's happiness and positive emotions, on physiology, stress, cognitive abilities and physical health, as well as on other harder-to-assess attributes, like 'self-actualization' and moral maturity"* (2007:251-2).

Fredrickson comments on the value of mindfulness: *"The power of mindfulness is that it can literally sever the link between negative thoughts and negative emotions. ... Perhaps the best way to develop the skill of mindfulness is to take a class or a workshop. ... Mindfulness training teaches people to do something that comes naturally and automatically with positive emotions. It teaches people to open their minds. When you practice mindfulness, instead of cultivating positivity directly, you make a beeline to openness. Yet because openness and positivity are fused- each causing and amplifying the other - your newly cultivated openness throws open the doors to positivity, creating the rush of the upward spiral"* (2009:167-8).

CONCLUSION

We saw in the previous chapter that "Broaden and Build" applies to the Four Immeasurables – each supports and reinforces the other three. The Positive Psychology themes introduced in this chapter do the same:

- Savouring links to Empathetic Joy – "May I enjoy things just as they are"
- Hope and Optimism are both features of the aspirations expressed for the Four Immeasurables, for example "May I be happy well and at peace"
- Forgiveness links strongly to Loving Kindness and Compassion
- Gratitude links to Empathetic Joy
- Challenging the Negativity Bias links to the 'four great efforts' outlined in Chapter One.

It is therefore fair to conclude that, just as the Four Immeasurables strengthen the benefits of mindfulness, so to do these ideas and practices from Positive Psychology, all of which relate well to the Four Immeasurables. This concludes the review of the content of Mindfulness Based Life Enhancement. It is now time to pull it all together, and this is the subject of the next chapter.

5. MINDFULNESS BASED LIFE ENHANCEMENT: THE COURSE

In this chapter we look at the integration of the themes identified in the previous chapter in Mindfulness Based Life Enhancement. We consider in more detail the key characteristics of this as a formal course, compare this to several other Mindfulness Based Interventions, and look at the teaching method involved, action learning. Finally, we explore the link of MBLE to wisdom.

This MBI draws upon 2500 years of experience in the East, but also on the extensive practice and research on mindfulness, compassion and positive psychology which has taken place in the West. It is designed both to reduce negative thinking (a fundamental objective in all Mindfulness Based Interventions) and to increase the positive, and is based on the premise that the positive and negative co-exist and interact. This approach therefore echoes Lander, who in his closing remarks to the Mind and Life Institute Conference in 2003, argued that while Buddhist practices emphasise attaining increased levels of mental awareness, modern science has focused on bringing patients to normalcy. *"Why stop there?"* he asked the audience. *"Why are we satisfied with saying we're not mentally ill? Why not focus on getting better and better?"*(quoted by Mingyur 2007:26).

In the Introduction I described the genesis of the MBLE course, which is now run in several formats [besides the eight week version below, there is also a six week version, involving sessions of 3 hours 15 minutes]. The course structure is summarised in Table 5.1, comparing the weekly themes with those provided by McCown et al (2010) in their MBSR metastructure, and showing how the additional themes come into the course. Besides my own experience, having participated in an eight-week course, as well as taking a Postgraduate Certificate in Mindfulness Based Approaches, and a Master of Science in Studies in Mindfulness, I also looked at relevant texts on MBSR, and sought ideas from other sources.

Theme	MBSR Curriculum	The Four Immeasurables	Positive Psychology
Table 5.1: MINDFULNESS BASED LIFE ENHANCEMENT			
1. Introducing Mindfulness & Automatic pilot	There's more right than wrong with you		Overview; Three key findings: Negativity bias; The 40% Solution; Broaden and Build
2. Acceptance	Perception and creative responding	Loving Kindness Meditation	Savouring
3. The Power of Being Present The Mindful Space	Pleasure and power of presence (pleasant events)	Compassion meditation	Hope
4. Thoughts are not facts Challenging Negative Thinking	Shadow of Stress (unpleasant events)	Empathetic Joy Meditation	Hope
5. Mindful Change	Finding space for responding	Equanimity Meditation	Gratitude
6. Cultivating patience and kindness the Four Immeasurables	Working with difficult situations	Meditation on the Four Immeasurables	Forgiveness (Self)

DAY OF PRACTICE	Sitting meditation; Walking meditation; Mindful Movement; Body Scan; Slow-Walking meditation; Mountain meditation; Four Immeasurables Meditation; Fast/slow walking; Dissolving the silence		
7. Relationships, Communication and Insight Dialogue	Cultivating kindness	The Four Immeasurables and Communication	Spirituality Strengths of Wisdom and Knowledge
8. Using what has been learned Life Enhancement by keeping your mindfulness alive	A new beginning		Happiness activities/ A new toolkit for positivity

The mindfulness dimension of the course followed closely the approach used in MBSR, incorporating all its basic practices. As McCown, Reibel and Micozzi state *"MBSR is not positioned as a clinical intervention at all, but rather as an educational program"* (2010:7), and it was therefore the natural base programme to adopt.

For mindful movement I took inspiration from the Maha-satipatthana Sutta, where the Buddha says: *"when walking, the monk discerns that he is walking. When standing, he discerns that he is standing. When sitting, he discerns that he is sitting. When lying down, he discerns that he is lying down"* (Walsh 1995:336). I drew on my practice of Pilates and Yoga to design three flowing sequences - Standing, Sitting and Lying - but emphasising that these were mindfulness practices, not exercise[36]. Together with Mindful Walking, these constitute the Mindful Movement aspects of the course. This sequencing has the additional

---

[36] I subsequently added movements from QiGong.

advantage that participants can do many of the Sitting Sequence movements at a desk - helpful to those who spend much of their working life in offices[37].

The themes drawn from Positive Psychology have been explored in the previous chapter. Their role in the course is summarised in Table 5.2, indicating the activities which participants are encouraged to follow each week.

Table 5.2: POSITIVE PSYCHOLOGY			
	Theme	Description	Activity
1	Negativity bias	The way humans give more weight to negative rather than positive experiences or information.	Look out for examples of this
2	The 40% Solution	"Half of happiness is "set" by genetics and 10% by "circumstances," leaving a full 40% subject to our constructive, creative, intentional activity." (Lyubomirsky 2007)	
3	Broaden and Build Theory	Positive emotions expand cognition and behavioural tendencies. (Frederickson 2009)	Consider your existing sense of positive emotions, and how these might be broadened and enhanced and look for ways of doing this as the course proceeds

---

[37] This also proved helpful for one course which included one person in a wheelchair, and two others who were unable to do sitting or lying mindful movement – they were encouraged to adapt the Sitting Movement sequence.

	Theme	Description	Activity
4	Savouring	Bryant's work on savouring is described, including ten strategies we can use to discover pleasure and satisfaction in everyday moments	Explore Savouring. Do the Savouring Vacation activity daily
5	Optimism	Quotations from several writers are used to describe optimism and its positive effects	Envision an airplane journey from an optimistic and a pessimistic perspective (Ricard 2007)
6	Hope	Quotations from several writers are used to describe hope and its positive effects	Dispute negative thoughts
7	Gratitude	Ten ways to become more grateful are outlined	Try the four gratitude exercises in the Guidebook
8	Forgiveness	The theme is introduced, and compared to related processes, including reconciliation	Consider whether there is anyone you want to consider forgiving, and explore the three activities in the Guidebook
9	Strengths of Wisdom and Knowledge	The 24 personal strengths identified by Seligman and Peterson are introduced	Do the questionnaire at the Authentic Happiness website

10	Happiness activities/A new toolkit for positivity	Summaries of recommended activities from the work of Lyubomirsky and of Frederickson are given and compared with the themes of the course	Choose your activities - and practice!

This, then, is the course. But how is it received by participants? Do they find it helpful, and if so in what way? This is the subject of the next Chapter, but first it is useful to consider how MBLE compares to other mindfulness courses. There are a growing number of courses which, like MBLE, have mindfulness as core, and are non-therapeutic. While these courses have very different origins and foci, they share some or all of the objectives set out in Chapter One.

AWAKENING JOY

This course is much longer than Mindfulness Based Interventions at eleven months, and is primarily internet based. The accompanying book (Baraz and Alexander 2010) identifies themes which include intention, mindfulness, gratitude, working with difficulties, learning to love oneself, and compassion. It will be seen that these themes resonate strongly with the wider canvas of MBLE. As Baraz describes it, "because I've been a teacher of Buddhist meditation for more than thirty years, many of the basic principles and time-tested practices in the Awakening Joy program come from that body of teachings. … However this is not a Buddhist course on happiness … its basic principles can be put into practice by anyone" (2010:xxi). Three of these principles are at the heart of the program:

1. Developing and Increasing Wholesome States
2. Focusing on the Gladness That Arises with Wholesome States
3. Inclining the Mind towards Wholesome States.

CULTIVATING EMOTIONAL BALANCE[38]

The Cultivating Emotional Balance research project began at the Mind and Life Institute event in 2000, where the Dalai Lama invited scientists to conduct research which might determine whether secularized Buddhist practices would be helpful to those dealing with "destructive" emotional experiences. Responding to this request, Ekman and Wallace developed "Cultivating Emotional Balance", which integrates Buddhist contemplative practices with Western techniques for dealing with negative emotional experiences[39].

Wallace identified three "Buddhist issues which could be presented in a secular fashion, open to all kinds of people"[40:]

- Shamatha attentional training
- Applying mindfulness to attending closely   four applications of mindfulness
- The Four Immeasurables.

This course has four key themes – Attentional, Conative, Cognitive and Affective Balance - and uses Tibetan medical diagnostics to identify in each case imbalance caused by deficit, hyperactivity or dysfunction. The course introduces participants to a variety of formal mindfulness practices, as well as considering the work on emotions by Ekman (2008). Attentional imbalance is addressed through the cultivation of mindfulness and introspection. Conative imbalance is addressed by consideration of the distinction between 'genuine happiness' (eudaemonia) and hedonic pleasure. Conative balance[41] is cultivated by:

---

[38] This account is based primarily on a workshop by B.Alan Wallace held at Kagyu Samy Dzong on 16-17 June 2012.

[39] http://www.cultivatingemotionalbalance.org/?q=node/9

[40] Quote from workshop.

[41] The conative "is one of three parts of the mind, along with the affective and cognitive. In short, the cognitive part of the brain measures intelligence, the affective deals with emotions and the conative drives how one acts on those thoughts and feelings." (http://en.wikipedia.org/wiki/Conation).

- Remedying apathy with recognition of the possibility of genuine happiness
- Remedying obsessive desire with the cultivation of contentment
- Remedying mistaken desires with recognition of the true causes of genuine happiness and of vulnerability to suffering.

Cognitive balance is cultivated through the Four Applications of Mindfulness (Body, Feelings, Mental States and Processes, and phenomena at large). Affective balance is cultivated through the Four Immeasurables:

- Remedy hedonism with loving-kindness
- Remedy aloof indifference with compassion
- Remedy depression with empathetic joy
- Remedy self-centred attachment with equanimity.

SEARCH INSIDE YOURSELF (GOOGLE)

Chade-Meng Tan, creator of Google's Search Inside Yourself course, began with MBSR, but as he commented to Shambhala Sun: "Stress reduction didn't really fly here." Google hires high achievers, and for them "stress can be a badge of honor, and not many people will sign on for stress reduction, particularly those who need it the most. So I needed to go beyond stress reduction. I wanted to help people find ways to align mindfulness practice with what they want to achieve in life, so they can create peace and happiness in themselves, and at the same time create world peace" (Shambhala Sun September 2009:34).

For Tan the key moment "came when I read Daniel Goleman's Emotional Intelligence. ... Reading that book gave me another epiphany. I had found my vehicle for aligning meditation with real life, and that vehicle is emotional intelligence ...... a very good way (and I suspect the only way) to truly develop EI is with contemplative practices starting with Mindfulness Meditation" (Tan 2012:234-5). The Search Inside Yourself Programme in Google has three steps:

- Develop Attention Training
- Increase Self Knowledge and Self Mastery
- Create Useful Mental Habits.

The Mindful Self-Compassion program developed by Neff and Germer[42] embraces both mindfulness and compassion. A randomized, controlled trial demonstrated that the MSC program significantly increased self-compassion, compassion for others, mindfulness, and life satisfaction, as well as decreased depression, anxiety and stress. Improvements were linked to how much a person practiced mindfulness and self-compassion in their daily lives. The program consists of eight, weekly, 2-hour sessions in a classroom/discussion group format, plus a 4-hour retreat. Themes of the sessions include:

- Discovering Mindful Self-Compassion
- Practising Mindfulness
- Practising Loving-Kindness Meditation
- Finding Your Compassionate Voice
- Living Deeply
- Managing Difficult Emotions
- Transforming Relationships
- Embracing Your Life.

THE PROCESS: ACTION LEARNING

The process used in the MBLE course is Reflective Experiential Action Learning. This is explained to participants:

The course is REAL: Reflective Experiential Action Learning (forgive my weakness for acronyms!) Action Learning has four stages:

- *Identifying the problems*
- *Identifying the causes of the problems*
- *Identifying the solution*
- *Putting into practice the solution.*

---

[42]During workshop at University of Derby, July 2012.

In an action learning set:

- *We learn from experience and share that experience with others*
- *We are open to the views of colleagues and listen to alternative suggestions*
- *We have time where we are listened to in a non-judgemental atmosphere*
- *We generate more choices about the way forward*
- *We review the outcome of actions with the support of fellow set members and share the lessons learned.*

In most action learning sets the action takes place outside the meeting. In this course it takes place also during each session, through formal and informal practices - hence the term Experiential. Thus the group will be working as an Action Learning set, reflecting on the experience you have during the sessions and in your home practice between the sessions, and hopefully through this drawing new insights into the practice.

Support for this way of using Action Learning is to be found in the writings of Revans, founder of action learning. When asked the origin of the ideas that inform it, he replied "they form the logical support to the teachings of the Buddha"(1992:534). Since the primary motivation of Mindfulness Based Interventions is the same as that espoused by the Buddha, this relationship is an important - and inspiring – one.

Table 5.3: ACTION LEARNING AND BUDDHISM
We may interpret the Four Noble Truths in the light of action learning theory as this has been presented in the modern literature. ...
The first: "This is suffering this have I declared"; it is the first principle of action learning that men (sic) learn only of their own volition, and not at the will of others.
The second truth: "This is the arising of suffering this have I declared." Our first task, having become aware of our suffering, is to identify its cause. Without diagnosis, without being able to recognise the arising of the problem, we cannot cure it.

The third noble truth set forth by the Buddha: "This is the cessation of suffering this have I declared", has its counterpart in action learning: the proposed solution to the problem that is the arising of the suffering.

It is, perhaps, the fourth truth enunciated by the Buddha that awakens the greatest interest in the student of action learning: "This is the path leading to the cessation of suffering this have I declared." It was he who, probably for the first time in the history of mankind, taught that salvation or at least deliverance from adversity must be achieved by each individual by his own actions.

Revans 1992, pp.535-538

During the course we seek to move through Heron's three modes of facilitation, the hierarchical, the participative and the autonomous (Figure 5-1), not least because "participants are encouraged to perceive session eight as the beginning of the rest of their life" (Crane 2009:96). As McCown et al say, "the teacher holds the treasures of the group in trust for the participants as they grow into the ability to care for those treasures by themselves" (2010:104). The three treasures they identify - freedom, belonging and resonance - can all be co-created within the medium of Reflective Experiential Action Leaning.

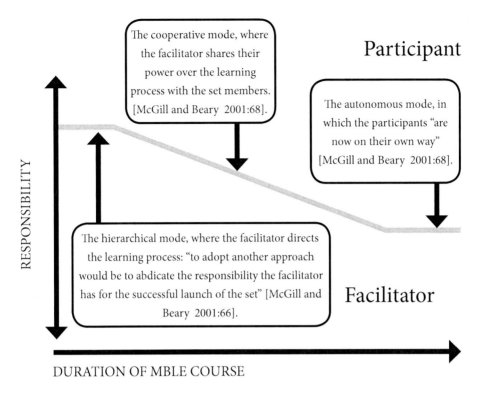

The cooperative mode, where the facilitator shares their power over the learning process with the set members. [McGill and Beary 2001:68].

Participant

The autonomous mode, in which the participants "are now on their own way" [McGill and Beary 2001:68].

The hierarchical mode, where the facilitator directs the learning process: "to adopt another approach would be to abdicate the responsibility the facilitator has for the successful launch of the set" [McGill and Beary 2001:66].

Facilitator

RESPONSIBILITY

DURATION OF MBLE COURSE

Figure 5-1: MODES OF FACILITATION

EXPERIENTIAL LEARNING

The emphasis on the course is on experiential learning – experiencing mindfulness, not talking about it. To achieve this, didactic exposition is limited to around 20 minutes in each session, excepting the first; the rest of the time is devoted to practice and (slowly increasing in time during the programme), small group and plenary discussion of first-person experience. The didactic material is contained in four Guidebooks, each covering two weeks, so that it is available to people as and when they want to learn more. These Guidebooks provide evidence in favour of mindfulness, outline Mindful Learning, explain the Four Immeasurables and the themes of positive psychology, and provide guidance to practice, as well as providing illustrative stories, quotations and poems. The Guidebooks are supplemented by a Home Activity Booklet describing activity each week. The choice of title is deliberate, avoiding the negative connotations often associated with 'Homework'. Each session therefore includes three major aspects - practice, discussion and exposition - with the balance gradually shifting each week so that there is increasing emphasis on discussion.

An additional factor was the role of language, highlighted in many treatments of Mindfulness Based Interventions (see for example Segal et al 2002:88-9). Drawing on Bateson (1973), Kolb (1984), and Honey and Mumford (1992) there are at least four learning styles:

- Reflectors, who like to observe and think things through
- Theorists, who like concepts and structure
- Pragmatists, who like to try things out
- Activists, who prefer concrete experience.

It is important to speak to each, and this applies particularly to the formal guided meditations, which need to use phrases which resonate with different learning styles.

LEARNING: THE FACILITATOR

Drawing on Rogers (1969), McGill and Beaty (2001:168-9) identify three core qualities of the facilitator, and add a fourth; they also reference the research done by Morgan (1988:189-90) who argued for four active facilitative skills. In terms of Mindfulness Based Interventions, the final one may be reinterpreted as the need to maintain a narrative flow for the course.

Core to the role of facilitator are the Four Immeasurables. There is a strong emphasis in the literature on teaching with Kindness and Compassion, and this can easily be extended to embrace the Four Immeasurables. Naming the course Life Enhancement was a deliberate emphasis on the positive, and savouring and gratitude complement Empathetic Joy. The facilitator can seek a lightness of approach which makes the sessions pleasurable, as well as challenging. And Equanimity is essential to the facilitator, providing balance and 'holding the space'.

Table 5.4: THE CORE QUALITIES AND ROLES OF THE FACILITATOR IN ACTION LEARNING	
	Source
The facilitator is genuine, real and congruent	Rogers
Acceptance and caring 'unconditional positive regard'	Rogers
Empathic understanding sensing accurately the feelings and meanings the facilitator is experiencing	Rogers
Creating a learning climate	McGill and Beaty
The need to manage group process, including group dynamics and time management	Morgan
The need to adopt a reflective, synthesising approach to group discussion	Morgan
The need to make interventions that 'frame' and 'reframe' the issues	Morgan
The need to make an unobtrusive record of the group discussion	Morgan

We can identify four key roles for a mindfulness teacher. The Architect sets the overall framework and provides the necessary supporting guidance and material. This links to McGill and Beaty's emphasis on creating a learning climate (2001:70). The Guardian ensures that the programme runs to time, as well as fostering an atmosphere of strong collective support where people are encouraged to practice, but not admonished when they do not. This relates to Morgan's facilitative role of managing group process. The Inspirer guides through example, and through developing in participants a confidence in the teacher's abilities. This relates to Roger's three qualities of the facilitator. Finally, the Facilitator embraces all the requirements identified above, as the skills of coach, mentor and encouraging learning to learn are all significant[43].

---

[43] It is no coincidence that one of the fastest growing areas of interest in mindfulness in organisations has been in the fields of coaching and mentoring.

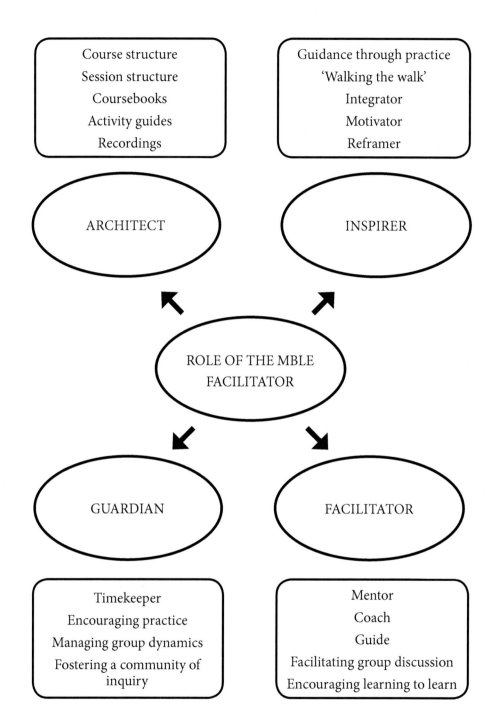

Figure 5-2: THE ROLE OF THE MBLE FACILITATOR

When teaching Mindfulness Based Interventions the goal is to practice all these roles in the spirit of the Four Immeasurables; for example, helping people to accept the difficulties which arise, advising against 'beating oneself up' when things don't seem to be going well, avoiding any guilt trips when home practice falls short, celebrating insights, and ensuring the overall content of the course is sufficient to provide people with the basis for future practice. Thus the mindfulness teacher needs to embrace Mindful Competence, bringing to bear their Expert Mind, but maintaining the Beginner's Mind that is willing to respond to comment, and at times 'unlearn' unhelpful practice. *"Previously learned group-work skills are likely to require modification, and indeed some unlearning may be necessary for the mindfulness model of practice"* (Melbourne Academic Interest Group, quoted in McCown et al 2010:105).

DEVELOPMENT: THE FIVE WISDOM FAMILIES

Besides mindfulness and the Four Immeasurables, in recent years a number of other ideas and practices drawn from Buddhist philosophy and psychology have been brought into Western thinking. Here we explore one example, the five Wisdom Families, also called the Wisdom Energies or the Buddha Families. To develop a picture of these we can usefully draw on four sources (Table 5.5). First, a popular treatment of the five has been provided by Rockwell (2002). Second, the Naropa Institute sees the Buddha Families as a "practical framework for balanced development and a foundation for lifelong learning" (McWilliams 1996.2). Third, Thrangu (2002), Chogyam Trungpa (Gimian 1999) and other Buddhist writers have explored these wisdoms within the Buddhist context, linking them to the eight consciousnesses and the five kinds of primordial awareness. Fourth, the Zen Center of Los Angeles (2012) and Green River Zen (2012:1) have developed them as "our own mandala of Five Practice Families" to enable them to "manifest in day-to-day life"[44].

---

[44] "At Zen Center, our signature ritual is "The Gate of Sweet Nectar," which is our weekly offering of feeding the hungry spirits. Part of this offering is the wisdom of the Five Buddha Families. We use these spheres to represent various functions of the Zen Center and specifically use the Mandala as the Circle of Life to orient folks to the Big Picture, rather than become too narrowly focussed in their own little spheres. In this way, we emphasize the practice of shared stewardship --linking, collaboration, effect of interconnectedness, and inviting forth the collective wisdom to serve the whole".

Table 5.5: WISDOM AND THE FIVE BUDDHA FAMILIES

	VAJRA	RATNA	PADMA	KARMA	BUDDHA
Thrangu	Mirrorlike	Equality	Discriminating	All-accomplishing	Dharmadhatu
Rockwell	Clarity	Richness	Passion	Activity	Spaciousness
Naropa	Clarity	Resourcefulness	Communication	Effective Action	Openness
GreenRiver Zen/ ZCLA	Study Wisdom of Mirror-like Seeing "See Clearly! "	Resources Wisdom of All-enriching Care "Take Care!"	Relationships Wisdom of Discriminating Awareness "Be Intimate and Bear Witness!"	Service: Wisdom of All-accomplishing action "Serve!"	Meditation/ Source: Empty-full: Wisdom of All-inclusiveness "Include everything - Don't Know!"

As a personal example of this, I have a strong Vajra personality, supplemented with Karma and, consequent on 25 years of meditation, Buddha has strengthened in me. Taking the qualities of Vajra identified by Rockwell: Mode: mental; Style: conceptual; Learning style: intellectual, using analysis, abstractions and general principles; Abilities of mind: having an overview, facility with logic and reasoning (my first Master's degree was in Mathematical Logic, while my Doctoral thesis addressed Complexity Theory and Fuzzy Logic). Intensified emotion: anger; Best time of day: dawn; Colour Blue; Passion: Wanting to know; Architecture: clean lines; Music: brilliant and clear (my favourite being Trance Euphoria). I have for years had two vajras and one double-vajra on my altar. And one of my first published articles on management was entitled Diamond Thunderbolt Management (1996).

Karma is to be seen in, for example, Environment: big, busy cities; Sane activity: Creating and carrying out projects; Visual art: Escher; Literature: How-to manuals. Buddha is shown in Visual art: minimalist, Japanese brush painting; Dance: American Indian; Literature: Haiku; Music: Philip Glass (I have almost everything he has composed); Spiritual style: Meditation; Learning style: Osmosis

My practice is now moving to a similar integration, and the Five Practice Families of Green River Zen have proved very helpful in setting perspective. Returning to the musical insight, Vajra/Karma/Buddha provide the plainchant, Ratna/Padma the soaring saxophone and it is the integration of them all that makes music/life joyful.

Helpful in this has been the greater use of visualisations. The latter are still new to me, partly because they have previously seemed alien compared with zazen, and partly because I considered myself very poor at visualisation. In this respect Thrangu's comment is very helpful: "Those who understand that each consciousness perceives in a different way know that mental images aren't as clear as the forms perceived with the eyes, and therefore they are content with their meditation" (2002:21). Where previously I would have seen inclusion of Tibetan practices as a dilution, I now see them as an enhancement.

Thus from Ratna comes richness: "In the positive expression of the Ratna family, the principle of richness is extraordinary. We feel very rich and plentiful, and we extend ourselves to our world personally, directly, emotionally, psychologically, even spiritually. ... The enlightened expression of Ratna is called the Wisdom of Equanimity, because Ratna can include everything in its expansive environment" (Chogyam Trungpa in Gimian 1999:164). From Padma comes passion: "In the awakened state, the heat of passion is transmuted into the warmth of compassion. When Padma neurosis is transmuted, it becomes fantastically precise and aware; it turns into tremendous interest and inquisitiveness. Everything is seen in its own distinct way, with its own particular qualities and characteristics. Thus, the wisdom of Padma is called Discriminating Awareness Wisdom" (ibid:165).

These experiences can in part be approached by adopting Rockwell's suggestion of gaining "an experiential sense of the quality of the Padma/Ratna family" (2002:49,59), for example by attending to clothing, environment, and music. We can relate this to savouring. As we have seen, this can involve the processes of cognitive reflection or experiential absorption (Table 4.7). The latter relates to richness and passion: absorption, behavioural expression, sharing with others, and sensory-perceptual sharpening, which they argue *may be a more effective strategy for enhancing the sensations that embody experiential absorption* (Bryant and Veroff 2007:137). A good example of this can be movement: besides approaching yoga and TaiChi classes with the intention of being mindful, one can also add the intention to luxuriate in the activity (and it works!). As Norbu comments *"Those who do breathing, yoga or dance exercises are especially adept at purifying their gross elements into light elements"* (2012:108).

There is however an important caveat to this: Bryant and Veroff argue that *"True wisdom lies in learning to savour in ways that achieve both hedonia and eudaimonia, without trading one form of happiness for the other"* (ibid:214). But what they identify as the 'potential cost' of luxuriating is narcissistic hedonism, paralleling Rockwell's identification of the 'neurotic activity' of Ratna as overindulgence, and of Padma as fantasizing and manipulating. To some extent the desired energy transformation can be seen as a shift from hedonic-focus to eudaimonic-focus.

We can take this further by using the Voice Dialogue method (Stone and Stone 1989a,1989b), which addresses the many energy patterns each person has, including the demonic energies which "are instinctual energies that have been disowned over time and have become destructive ... What is remarkable about this whole process is that when we have the courage to look at our disowned parts, they change. ... Voice Dialogue can be viewed as a tool similar to meditation. ... but we are focusing on the energies we can reach using the dialogue process and some levels of visualization" (1989a:67, 79, 143, 231).

The term 'transformation' is problematic, but here we can take again the example of anger, and draw guidance from Thrangu Rinpoche, adopting the notion of "completely purified anger ... due to the realization of the true nature, the primordial awareness is seen in the affliction" (2002:76,104). This purification has an additional dimension, inspired by Khandro Rinpoche, who told a student that "Anger is always a waste of time", and when the student was shocked by this, continued "I didn't tell you to give up your critical intelligence. I told you anger is a waste of time" (quoted in Gross 2006:232).

Thrangu argues that there are "four causes for attaining primordial awareness: ... Though in general there are five kinds of primordial awareness, since the primordial awareness of the dharmadhatu pervades all the others, only four causes for the attainment of primordial awareness are taught." (Thrangu 2002:57-8). This provides an interesting link to Zen, through the "four ways of knowing and true awakening" knowing of the Great Perfect Mirror, Equality, by Differentiation, and Perfection of Action - which Hakuin links to four gates on the Buddhist path: the Gates of Inspiration, Practice, Awakening, and Nirvana (Low 2006:30-39). As Richmond argues, there is "a strong resonance and affinity between the Mahamudra and Zen traditions"[46], and with Lama Palden he has been developing this, starting with "The Heart Sutra as a vitally important text for both traditions"[47].

---

[46] http://www.zenheartvajraheart.com/index.php?option=com_content&view=article&id=8&Itemid=5

[47] ibid

THE FIVE WISDOM FAMILIES AND MBLE

The Five Wisdom Families have proved helpful in refining the MBLE course, in particular in relation to the desire to use language and practice which would reach all (Table 5.6). The initial preparation of the course, designing all the elements, creating the structure - all these drew on my three strongest families, Vajra, with Buddha/Karma subsidiary. As I have developed the course I have added aspects of my weakest families, Padma/Ratna - more poetry and music for example, and greater focus on the creation of a community of practice. And while my 'home three' are important in delivery, Padma/Ratna prove to be the best mindsets through which to teach the course itself, with their stress on resources, communication and relationships.

Table 5.6: THE ROLE OF THE WISDOM FAMILIES IN MINDFULNESS BASED LIFE ENHANCEMENT			
	Content	**Preparation**	**Delivery**
Buddha	Mindfulness	Preparation of texts for guided meditations	Leading guided meditations
Vajra	Mindful Learning	Overall design of the programme	Ensuring the design is effectively implemented
Ratna	Positive Psychology	Inclusion of poetry and music	Providing a rich experience
Ratna	Four Immeasurables	Inclusion of opportunities for collective reflection and discussion	Creating a community of practice and encouraging mindful communication and dialogue
Karma	Mindful Movement	Attention to the physical needs of participants	Leading mindful movement activities

6. IS MINDFULNESS BASED LIFE ENHANCEMENT EFFECTIVE?

> In this Chapter we explore the effectiveness of MBLE as judged by more than 100 participants in the first ten courses.

INTRODUCTION

In evaluating MBLE it has been important to establish:

1. If MBLE provide the benefits of conventional Mindfulness Based Interventions, in particular MBSR.
2. If the addition of Mindful Learning, the Four Immeasurables and Positive Psychology to the course content provide added benefits to participants.
3. What contribution Action Learning brings to teaching mindfulness in group settings, both for the teacher and for the group.

McCown et al's identification of five learning outcomes is helpful when exploring the benefits to participants (2010:143). These are:

- Experiencing new possibilities (reframing)
- Discovering embodiment (introception and proprioception)
- Cultivating the observer (reperceiving)
- Moving towards acceptance (of what is always changing and what cannot be changed)
- Growing compassion.

The fifth, Growing compassion, "reveals itself, at first implicitly and mostly directed towards the self, and later, explicitly and extended towards the other as well as the self"(2010:146). In Mindfulness Based Life Enhancement these five are also present, but Growing Compassion (or more precisely, Growing the Four Immeasurables) is explicit from the start for both self and other. There are two further learning outcomes: Cultivating Mindful Change, introduced in Week Five, and Enhancing the Quality of Life (Figure 6-1).

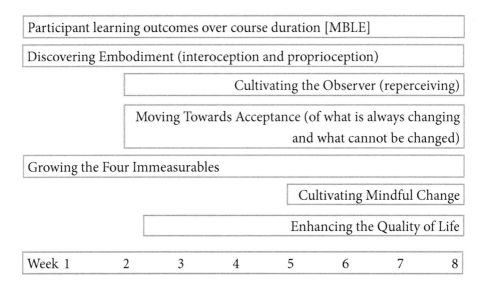

PARTICIPANT LEARNING OUTCOMES OVER COURSE DURATION[MBLE]							
Participant learning outcomes over course duration [MBLE]							
Discovering Embodiment (interoception and proprioception)							
				Cultivating the Observer (reperceiving)			
			Moving Towards Acceptance (of what is always changing and what cannot be changed)				
Growing the Four Immeasurables							
						Cultivating Mindful Change	
						Enhancing the Quality of Life	
Week 1	2	3	4	5	6	7	8

Figure 6-1: PARTICIPANT LEARNING OUTCOMES OVER COURSE DURATION: MBLE

EVALUATING THE COURSE

As the intention has been to evaluate both the overall content of MBLE, and the course itself, a number of interrelated evaluation methods were used. These included:

- First Person Experience: personal reflection after each session on how it had gone, what worked and what needed amendment, as well as my role as teacher/facilitator. Here I used an action research methodology which led to many minor improvements, for example:
  - More discussion of acceptance.
  - A greater emphasis on the key point that the practices are intended to deepen qualities such as gratitude and compassion. We all have these within us, and MBLE helps to reveal them where hidden, and to deepen and enhance them.

- Participants in the first courses indicated they would like more time for group discussion. To allow this, sessions were extended by 15 minutes[48].
- More discussion of Mindful Movement, as well as greater use of Qigong.
- The addition of Tonglen as an explicit practice.

- Community of Inquiry: learning from participants what they found helpful, what they found difficult, what needed more explanation, what needed more time, what additions or subtractions needed consideration. Each course concludes with a discussion based on Revans' action learning approach, as well as evaluation forms exploring what participants liked and did not like, what they have found useful, what impact the course has had on their everyday lives. A number of participants have also answered follow-up questionnaires on the longer term impact of the course on them. This has been helped by the development of an 'alumni' group, who are invited to monthly continuation sessions.

- The colleague from whom I sought advice on Positive Psychology is an experienced researcher, and she offered at the outset to do independent evaluation of the first two courses.

EVALUATING THE BENEFITS TO PARTICIPANTS
ACTION LEARNING BY THE GROUPS

At the end of each course participants are asked to consider their answers to the four Action Learning Questions, which are deliberately left ambiguous (for example, is it the problems that brought them to the course, or the problems they have identified during the course?). This is to keep the range of answers as open as possible. It became apparent that my expectations were far too neat and structured. I envisaged answers such as 'habitual styles of thinking

---

[48] Timing has been an important area of variability in Mindfulness Based Interventions: McCown and Reibel (2009:10) report that three issues in particular are the length of the course, duration of class sessions, and duration of home practice sessions. Several studies report class durations of 1-1/2 to 2 hours (Astin, 1997; Jain et al, 2007; Roth & Calle-Mesa, 2006; Rosenzweig et al., 2003).

and acting', 'skilled incompetence', 'awareness of emotions and feelings', and reference to the formal meditations. Participants' answers were much more fluid, linking the four questions in rich variety, as shown in Table 6.1.

Table 6.1: THE FOUR ACTION LEARNING QUESTIONS, AND PARTICIPANTS' RESPONSES	
What are the problems?	
• Focussing on the future • Monkey mind not able to concentrate • Inner conditioning about what is a priority • Wanted help in removing self-imposed hairshirt	• Too busy thinking about what we should/ought/must do and feeling there isn't time to do them • Never having enough time • Getting irritated with those who are not fast
What are the causes of these problems?	
• Not living in the present • Getting anxious, and caught up in the anxiety • Being unaware of thoughts, and the impacts • Bad outweighing the good • Not aware of the choice to do things differently • Not savouring • Not seeing things as they really are	• Guilt • Idea that we need to go into our heads • Fast pace of modern life • Stress • Seeing other people's needs as more important than ours • Too much multi-tasking

What are the solutions?	
• Focussing on the moment and the breathing • Acceptance • Letting go particularly of unnecessary worry • Forgiveness and Self-forgiveness • Dispute negative thinking • Showing gratitude • Noticing / awareness • Give myself permission to do a constructive nothing	• Sharing as appropriate • Compassion to myself • Thinking before acting • Not worrying about things you can't change • Being less controlling and more trusting • Be more mindful in everything you do • Suspending judgement and being compassionate • Accept it as it is now • Listening to myself and acting on it
What are the practices and actions that help in the solutions?	
• Formal and informal practice • Lake and mountain meditations • Yoga • Loving Kindness • Savouring including the 'Daily Vacation Activity' • Smiling • Not thinking about it too much • Bodyscan listening to and connecting with the body	• The two darts • Mindfulness in the moment • Equanimity - holding good and bad • Poetry and music • Recognising other people have their baggage • Listing the good and coming back to these when things are not so good • Having space and allowing it for others

Although addressed in many different ways, participants embrace the key themes of the course, identifying concerns, causal links, and practical solutions. We can also see, moving through the four questions, a shift from the negative to the positive. Returning to the link between Action Learning and the Four Noble Truths identified by Revans, the Truths concern dukkha (suffering, anxiety, dissatisfaction), its origin, its cessation, and the path leading to its cessation. The groups' answers to the questions imply a parallel summary:

- The problem: our everyday state of life: anxiety, stress, negative thinking, busyness, lack of time, overcommitment, anxiety
- The cause: the second dart, negative emotions, external factors, background, history and upbringing, mindlessness, habit, harmful emotions
- The remedy: acceptance, compassion, mindful space, gratitude, forgiveness, cultivating mindfulness and beneficial emotions
- The way to achieve this: Mindfulness Based Life Enhancement, with savouring and mindful movement particularly mentioned.

Integrating these many responses, it is possible to recast MBLE as eight closely interlinked practices:

1. Practising formal and informal mindfulness
2. Challenging negative thinking through mindful learning
3. Enhancing kindness and compassion
4. Enjoying life and savouring
5. Enhancing balance and equanimity
6. Enriching optimism and hope
7. Practising gratitude and forgiveness
8. Engaging in mindful movement and somatic awareness.

So this activity shows participants in each course have realised the Learning Outcomes identified in Figure 6-1. They have identified new possibilities, enhanced embodiment, cultivated observation and moved toward acceptance. And they have enhanced their understanding and experience of the Four

Immeasurables and the qualities from Positive Psychology. We shall return to these eight interlinked practices in the final chapter, showing how they provide a framework for life enhancement.

THE EFFECT ON PARTICIPANTS: MINDFULNESS

At the conclusion of each course participants are given a short evaluation questionnaire, and the following discussion draws on more than 100 responses. Here are some of the responses:

- *As a result of the course my energy levels have gone up, I am able to focus better on the task at hand (both at work and at home). I am able to relax and I am more aware of my thoughts. I aim to continue with the practices and relaxation exercises I have learnt over the course which will hopefully develop lifelong skills for the future.*
- *It really did make a difference at a difficult time and continues to do so. It's made me more aware of lots of things.*
- *I felt the benefits straight away and found after a while my concentration levels had improved.*
- *This course has been very insightful and taught me how important it is to value myself and to stop for a while and smell the roses.*
- *I have had a virus which has prevented me from doing my usual activities which nourish and distress me. Without this course I would have found it very difficult to manage my work load and emotional responses to my clients' trauma.*
- *I found the course excellent and very life changing. Though I was aware of most (but not all) of the principles, I found that by learning with others in a group, that I will carry on using what I have learnt, and have incorporated meditation into my daily life in addition to my yoga.*

When asked: Can you give examples of the effect of mindfulness on your everyday life?, comments include *"Calmer, more present in the moment, more alive, more aware, less reactive, more mindful, informal mindfulness, more thoughtful, more patient with myself, rushing about less, acceptance of things as they are, tending to eat with more relish, more conscious of what is going on in my head, more of a feeling of calmness and taking each moment at a time".*

Follow-up surveys have indicated lasting benefits: *"more confident, reduced anxiety, increased focus, more aware, more content, communicating more mindfully, more self-aware, in touch with my body, living more often in the present moment".* Asked to give examples of the effect of mindfulness, respondents mention: *"less fearful, better work-life balance, taking time to reflect, exercising more, more patient, heightened awareness, calm in this turbulent world, 'becoming the person you are intended to be', a sense of calm".*

Other comments include:

- *It is still a surprise when stillness and meditation and deep breathing can have such a profound effect on how I see things.*
- *The course on mindfulness has been life-changing. It has taught me lifelong skills that have had a positive impact on my health, wellbeing and ability to perform at work.*
- *I wish I had found it thirty years ago, but am grateful that I have discovered it now. I look forward to the enrichment it will bring to my life in the future, as I develop my practice.*
- *I feel that I have been able to take what felt right for me from the course and integrate it into my everyday life. I have a feeling that if I had particular crises or stresses, mindfulness would now be one of the first ways I would think of helping myself cope as it has become part of my everyday life.*
- *The course really helped me to get back on track, becoming more centred, resilient and less self-pitying. It helped empower me to address the social isolation I was experiencing due to being a carer 7 days a week.*

THE EFFECT ON PARTICIPANTS: THE FOUR IMMEASURABLES AND POSITIVE PSYCHOLOGY

Participants are asked: Can you give examples of the effect of the Four Immeasurables on your everyday life? Answers to this question are mixed. Several people comment 'Not yet' or 'I'm not sure I can'. But the majority are positive, and include:

- *I feel these are already very integral to my natural approach anyway, but have increased my conscious awareness of my expression of them.*
- *More patience with Mum, partner and self. Greater pleasure in the little things. More humour. More energy. More ability to deal with things/people.*
- *The course enhanced my own belief in manifesting such qualities on a daily basis - these virtues should be practiced and put into actions all the times.*
- *Loving kindness has helped me be stronger asking for what I need and therefore how to be happier.*
- *Loving kindness to my partner, compassion for him too, when he gets it wrong!*
- *I would like to think I possessed these qualities before but am now more conscious of them and more mindful of how I relate to others.*

These comments reiterate the importance of presenting these as qualities to be enhanced, rather than created. Participants were also asked what they found most and least helpful about the aspects of positive psychology introduced on the course. There were many positive[49], and few negative, comments, with savouring and gratitude particularly popular. Follow-up surveys show that a number of participants continue to find these helpful in the practice of informal mindfulness, citing savouring, tuning into breathing, gratitude, and mindful eating.

One of the most interesting discoveries was that the themes introduced merged in people's minds with other themes in the course. Thus in answer to this question, several people mentioned the Two Darts metaphor, as well as the automatic pilot, the mountain meditation and compassion.

---

[49] No pun intended!

HOME PRACTICE

Doing home practice is always a major issue for participants. From an early stage in the course people are 'confessing' that they are not doing it as requested, and while this leads to some valuable discussion about the importance of 'not beating yourself up', the central role of home activity made this a matter of concern. McCown and Reibel report that "There is no consensus on the relationship between home practice duration or frequency and health outcomes" (2009:10), but there is no challenge to the argument that it should be part of the course. To help address this, I created two suites of short meditations (5-minute and 10-minute), and encourage participants to use these as a minimum each day.

THE CONTRIBUTION OF ACTION LEARNING

Participants are asked: **How did you find your experience of learning about mindfulness in a group? What were the advantages and disadvantages?** The response is overwhelmingly positive:

- *Excellent. It's useful to be part of a supportive group.*
- *Very positive. I thought the group dynamic was good and conducive to learning about mindfulness.*
- *I enjoyed the group and exchanging experiences with others.*
- *Really good. I felt very comfortable in the group. It was interesting to get different views, and appreciate that we were all there for different reasons - but we were all there.*
- *Useful insights provided by group members and mutual support.*
- *It is really helpful to be in a group.*
- *I like the group vibe, and group encouragement. It was good to hear that others were having similar experiences.*
- *Ideal, the perfect way for me to learn.*
- *I am someone who can find this type of group difficult, but because of the relaxed way in which you ran the group I liked learning in this way. So advantage for me was the learning from others and sharing experiences, especially in the small groups.*

- *I find it very, very helpful being in a group. There is a sharing, a sense of everyone coming together with a common purpose (even if there are variations on that).*

Overall, it is reasonable to conclude from this evidence that the action learning approach is an appropriate approach to take in non-clinical settings.

INDEPENDENT ASSESSMENT

As stated earlier, a colleague offered to do independent evaluation of course effectiveness, using before and after self-assessment reports based on the five facets (Baer, Smith, Hopkins, Krietemeyer and Toney 2006). There were 19 completed data sets for analysis for mindfulness at the end of the course evaluation and 23 completed for the other measures.

The results from the first two courses were as shown below; the commentary is by the independent evaluator. *"Comparison of means scores before the course began and at the end of the course using a two-tailed paired t-test with a Bonferroni correction factor[50] suggested that there were significant increases in several components of mindfulness and psychological strengths (Table 6.2, Table 6.3). After the course, participants displayed significant increase in their scores on all the components of mindfulness apart from mindfulness describing/ labelling with words. Scores on gratitude, both components of hope and self-forgiveness all increased significantly. There were no significant differences in scores for optimism and other forgiveness. This evaluation therefore provides further evidence that MBLE contributes to enhanced mindfulness."*

---

[50] The Bonferroni correction is a simple way to adjust for multiple comparisons. Perform each test at significance level α. Multiply each p-value by the number of tests performed. The overall significance level (chance of any of the tests rejecting in error) will be less than α.

Table 6.2: INCREASES IN MINDFULNESS STRENGTHS		
	t(19)	p
Total mindfulness	3.591	.01
Mindfulness: observing/noticing /attending to sensations, thoughts, feelings	2.81	.01
Mindfulness: acting with awareness/not on automatic pilot	3.91	.001
Mindfulness: non-judging of inner experience	2.93	.01
Mindfulness: non reactivity to inner experience	3.01	.01
The difference in Mindfulness describing/ labelling with words was not significant t(19)=.924). This may be explained perhaps by a having a sample that are already very good at verbal labelling.		

Table 6.3: INCREASES IN PSYCHOLOGICAL STRENGTHS		
	t(22)	p
Gratitude	2.59	.05
Hope Agency	2.77	.01
Hope Pathways	2.02	.05
Self-forgiveness	3.57	.01
The difference in optimism was not significant t(22) = .98) nor was the difference in other-forgiveness t(22)= 1.61		

CONCLUSION

The integrity of MBLE is reinforced by the evidence that participants experience the course holistically - they do not see the variations as 'add-ons', but integrate them in ways appropriate to themselves. I recognise that a third-person evaluation comparing the initial running of the course with the current iteration is not possible, but my first-person experience is that there has been a progressive shift. This is supported by the feedback - for example, the increased satisfaction with the time given to discussion, and the changing view of the Four Immeasurables. It is to the latter that we now turn.

7. UNDERSTANDING THE ROLE OF THE FOUR IMMEASURABLES

In this Chapter we look further at the important role that the Four Immeasurables play in Mindfulness Based Life Enhancement. This raises the question of how these four qualities relate to values expressed in various traditions. The chapter outlines the results of hermeneutic research undertaken to explore this, incorporating also discussion of the aspects of Positive Psychology brought into MBLE, and their relationship to the Four Immeasurables.

It is essential that the Four Immeasurables are presented and practiced in a way that uses language and approaches which speak to all. This means it is worth identifying possible constraints for particular groups, including areas of dissonance between the approach taken and values expressed by respondents, and solutions to those constraints.

I addressed this question through hermeneutic research[51], involving interviews with eight people, drawn from several faiths, but including two without religious belief. Six had been on the MBLE course; the other two were University Chaplains. The faiths were Christian (Anglican, Catholic and Quaker), Orthodox Jewish, Baha'i, and Moslem Sufi. While the focus of these interviews was on the Four Immeasurables, what emerged also was the close relationship of these to the themes from Positive Psychology which are also part of MBLE. The following discussion reflects this by considering eleven themes under three broad heading – the Four Immeasurables, Positive Psychology, and Interrelationships. We also consider briefly the Buddhist context – is this in any way an impediment to those approaching MBLE from a different spiritual background [whether or not in the form of organised religion]?

---

[51] The hermeneutic process seeks to uncover the meanings held by people about themselves, their ideas and their values. It therefore emphasises subjective interpretations and the individual's own world view.

THE FOUR IMMEASURABLES

LOVING-KINDNESS AND COMPASSION

All respondents characterised loving-kindness and compassion in ways consistent with their use in the MBLE course. This is important, since in western treatments compassion is often seen as equivalent to pity. Thus the American Heritage Dictionary gives pity, compassion and empathy as synonyms[52]. But in Buddhaghosa's treatment of the Four Immeasurables (1956) pity is the Near Enemy of compassion - a quality that can masquerade as the original, but is not the same, characterised as it is by inequality. Respondents took a similar view:

Loving Kindness and Compassion
Compassion doesn't mean feeling sorry for people, but trying to accept them for how and what they are and trying to have an understanding. Compassion has to come with understanding other individuals and their situations.
The Greek word for compassion in the New Testament is linked to the word for bowels so it is about being moved to the absolute depths of your being, it is much more than an intellectual feeling that there is someone suffering and it would be good for us to do something.
Compassion is walking alongside people having a hard time, and trying to see there is more to somebody than the problem they have got at the moment or their difficulties or struggles of life.
Compassion is basically not only the ability to stand in somebody else's shoes, which is probably just empathy, but compassion goes beyond that and entails feeling what the other person is likely to be feeling.

---

[52] http://www.ahdictionary.com/word/search.html?q=pity (Accessed 5 December 2012)

> Before I did the course I saw it in a more general way as feelings about other people in their situation, but since I have done the course I define it in a more specific way of relating to individual people around me who are having may be a hard time, and I think about what I might do to help them with what they are going through.

> I feel that compassion is being alongside somebody who is suffering in some way. It's not identifying with that person or their pain or distress, but it's being present to what is happening for him or her, and my own needs my own self and wants aren't getting in the way.

EMPATHETIC JOY

Unlike Loving-Kindness/Compassion, Empathetic Joy is not readily understood. This was reinforced when several respondents asked for my definition, although all were then able to articulate their own understanding. What emerged was the need to disaggregate the concept. Joy - a positive delight in life - is straightforward, and readily links to themes such as loving-kindness and gratitude. The importance of seeking this for both self and others is also readily understood. Thus these need to be introduced separately and then integrated.

Empathetic Joy
Empathy is something that I understand - it is being in somebody else's shoes, resonating with somebody else's feelings.
You have to really and sincerely feel happy for other people's achievements and also encourage them because you would like them to encourage you - so you have to treat others in the way that you think, but you have to remember to be like that.

I think it's to do with happiness, being contented with life. You do have people who have a certain amount of suffering or sickness or whatever who still have a certain amount of joy and joyfulness about them as well, so it doesn't mean that everything is OK. You can be joyful even in life's difficulties as well.

I think (loving-kindness) is just generally having a generous disposition towards other people and if you adopt that attitude it does make you feel happier. That was something I found very useful because the idea that you can rejoice in somebody else's gain or success, I think it is quite alien to our society. … so I think that idea of Empathetic Joy is very positive because it increases your net happiness and again it helps you to feel happier generally and if you can express that empathic joy to the person, if you know them, you can express it, it does them good, and I find that it can be responded to. The positive joy in other people's experience is something that I hadn't been aware of which I practice now.

I would define this as being pleased when other people are taking pleasure in their happiness and trying to add to it but also it makes you feel happy as well when other people are happy, when your friends are happy, it rubs off on you. And what about that toward yourself? Yes this would be taking pleasure in quite small things. And allowing yourself to have the time to experience them and rather than just rushing on and thinking this is a waste of time, being joyful about something that is happening around you and losing the guilt feeling about enjoying it.

EQUANIMITY

This too is a difficult concept, but when characterised as 'balance' proves more accessible. In the Four Immeasurables the phrase often used is "May I be free from preference and prejudice"[53]. "Free from preference" proves a problematic issue on the MBLE course if interpreted as suggesting we should be free from all preferences (e.g. of one person over others, or trivially, of coffee over tea). But when understood as bias - preferring my people to yours - it is more clearly linked to prejudice.

Equanimity
I think the wider definition of this is 'all beings don't tread on an ant' sort of thing. I have become much more aware of that. So we allowed a wasps' nest to develop in the house rather than killing it off and when I see spiders around the house I wish them good luck.
In the Baha'i faith all kinds of prejudice should be eliminated from our thoughts and our minds and our actions because prejudice actually will come in so many different shapes and meanings.
I think that would link very much with the notion of the whole of humanity being created in the image of and the likeness of God. .... And that should lead to a real passion and concern for justice. For justice that extends to all people.
As human beings we all have rights, the right for a peaceful life, for justice. We are all equal in the sight of god.
Well that is kind of feeling balance. And not letting anything upset you too much and at the same time not being overly joyous about something. It's like having an appropriate sense of commitment and an appropriate sense of detachment.

---

[53] See for example The Unfettered Mind http://www.unfetteredmind.org/practices/includes/ immeasurables-prayer.pdf (Accessed 6 December 2012)

> Before I did the course I defined that much more stoically, putting up with whatever life threw at you, it was something to be endured. Whereas now I see it as something which is much more in my control, I can do things which I know will make me feel equanimity towards myself and the way I behave in my environment.

> I experience equanimity as a space where I am approaching the situations as if for the first time, so I am not going in with my head full of assumptions or prejudices or ideas about how it's going to be or how I wanted to be. It's a non-judgmental attitude which opens me up to the bigger picture, it enables me to hold polarities and be open to different perspectives.

> I think (the course) just made them much more focused and particularly equanimity and I think it really heightened my awareness of trying to go into situations with no assumptions, and it does help me a lot to think of that. We can be very judgmental.

Thus people have a tacit understanding of both Empathetic Joy and Equanimity, and it is possible therefore to use Nonaka and Takeuchi's (1995) model of Knowledge Conversion to identify how to improve the treatment of these in MBLE. They drew on Polanyi's (1958) distinction between tacit knowledge, which is embodied (knowledge of experience), and explicit knowledge, which is codified (knowledge of rationality). From this distinction they develop their model of knowledge creation/conversion through a spiralling process of interactions (Figure 7-1). People already have a Sympathised Knowledge of these virtues. By introducing them explicitly during the course (Conceptual Knowledge), people can combine and integrate them with their existing values (Systemic Knowledge) and thus embed them more strongly into their practice and behaviour (Operational Knowledge).

KNOWLEDGE CONVERSATION

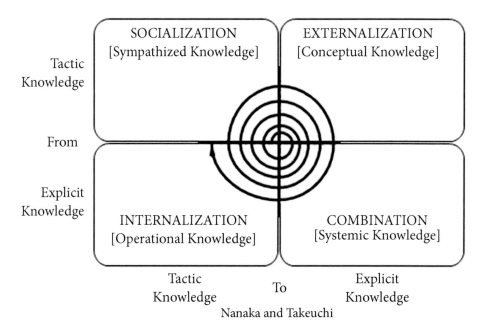

Nanaka and Takeuchi

Figure 7-1: KNOWLEDGE CONVERSION

POSITIVE PSYCHOLOGY

GRATITUDE

Gratitude emerges as an important value and practice for the self in enhancing positive feelings about life, and for others in expressing interconnection. Like other themes in MBLE, the issue is not persuading people to adopt it: they already know and express it. But an explicit focus on the value leads to new insights, and enhancement of its role.

Gratitude
I was sitting in front of my Sheikh years ago and I suddenly felt so happy and grateful for everything and I didn't know how to express it. I had a baby or two by then and I was married, and everything was so clear and I was grateful in my heart.
Personally I like to be grateful at every moment and every day and at every moment I need to remember to be grateful … you thank God for so many things.
It is quite important in our tradition to recognise the giftedness of life, the giftedness of other people, and to be grateful for that.
I certainly think that gratitude is very important. A lot of people don't think it's very important, they don't think that saying thank you is important. But saying thanks can actually be very good for the person who says it and it is very good for the recipient. I exercise by going for a walk, and instead of taking an iPod with me and listening to music I look at the trees and the fields and the sky and I think what a nice world that is and how lucky I am to have this environment, and to be healthy enough to walk in it.
I count my blessings. And I sort of renew that in terms of being continually thankful for the same things. It can appear that I go over and over the same things but for me it means there are a lot of key building blocks and I constantly think about them and I am grateful that they are OK and I revisit them and sometimes I have new ones.
Gratitude, that's changed in a big way. I especially liked the exercise[54] about gratitude sort of thinking about quite small things but also the huge pleasure that you can get from being grateful for small things, and that's made me feel much more appreciative, particularly of nature. I think I was quite appreciative of nature but I am even more appreciative of it.

---

[54] On the MBLE course

Forgiveness emerged from this research as more significant than originally expected. While there is an extensive discussion of this in the MBLE Coursebook[55], the interviews (supported by feedback from course participants) indicate that it needs to be explicitly treated. And like the Four Immeasurables this needs to apply to both self and others. The close relationship between compassion and forgiveness is one illustration of the way in which the Four Immeasurables and values from Positive Psychology interlink and reinforce each other.

Forgiveness
Forgiveness is a hard one. I think forgiveness has to come because sometimes maybe something happens, maybe you have been hurt by someone. You might not forget it and I think if you don't forget it, it is fine, but I think forgiveness is one of the strongest divine virtues, and you truly have to exercise it to the full sense.
I think we shouldn't be too forgiving to ourselves. You need to be kind to yourself and think that this life has been given to you - God has created you out of his love, so we have to really think about it as a very precious thing and really try to live your life according to what you think you should.
The Lord's Prayer is one of the key texts and the middle of the text goes 'forgive us our trespasses or our sins as we forgive those who trespass against us'. Forgiveness is a core teaching within Christianity. I think that any Christian would comment on how difficult that actually is to live out in practice.

---

[55] Provided by a colleague who has studied the issue in depth.

I remember a Russian Orthodox Bishop, he tells the story about being asked by an elderly lady once, she came to him and said she's got this real problem, every time I pray the Lord's Prayer, I get to that point and I say 'forgive us our trespasses as we forgive those who trespass against us', and I can't say the second part, and she would recount this story about this terrible thing that had happened to her. He said to her when you get to that point instead of praying that second part, just say forgive us our trespasses as one day I hope to find it in my heart to forgive so and so, and he made it achievable for her, and in a sense gave her a direction to travel rather than to feel that she could move from there to there just like that.

I think joy is something that that you wish for people, you want for people. I think it comes when you have forgiven, and when you forgive yourself.

Forgiveness is very important in Judaism because of the Day of Atonement which is the holiest day of the year and it is a day of repentance, a day of fasting and constant prayer where we are asking God to forgive us for the sins that we have committed in the previous year.

With forgiveness, instead of waiting till the Day of Atonement for the period between the first of the new year and the 10th day to consciously forgive people, I am more forgiving generally in the sense that if I feel that somebody has wrong to me, I will think well they're only human and you can't expect too much from people, and maybe in their shoes I would do the same thing.

I suppose self-forgiveness is the hardest thing for me. I try to be more forgiving towards myself. But don't always succeed, but at least I am aware that it is an issue.

HOPE AND OPTIMISM

Although these are treated separately in Positive Psychology, they emerged here as closely interrelated - several participants discussed them together. They also provided important linkages to people's wider belief systems. I had already concluded, before this research, that 'conative balance' needed to be explicitly addressed[56], giving people the opportunity to consider purpose and meaning in their lives. The interviews reinforced this view, but also indicated that this could be done by explicitly encouraging people to relate the values to their existing value system, and once again the focus is on enhancing what already exists.

Hope and Optimism
Hope is really important in Islam.
What I have learned though with all of these things is that you have to do it, you can't just be optimistic and hope things will just happen.
Hope is also linked to faith.
Christian hope is premised on a conviction that this life is not the end, that there is a greater life that is yet to come, and our life on earth is not just a sort of pale imitation. That is not to diminish the significance of life on earth but our belief is that we are actually part of something that our life continues.
In our Catholic or Christian tradition the great hope is the hope of the resurrection, the life and death of Jesus and we believe that Jesus rose from the dead, but in our own life we hope for resurrection.
The ideas of optimism and hope are not expressly indicated but the whole essence of prayer or serving God, the idea is that things will be okay and you'll be cared for.

---

[56] Conative balance is one of the four emotional balances in the course developed by Wallace and Ekman, discussed earlier.

That's a bit of a strange concept, hope. I suppose I define it in the sense of optimism, I mean hope I would use in the context of things being awful and they've got to get better, and being quite a sort of powerless emotion, and I might use the emotion in terms of thinking about truly dreadful things happening in other countries.

I think the positive psychology, I think that really helped me, what we did on the course because the visual diagram, that 50% is genetic, 40% you can do something about, 10% environment, I think that impacted me because it was in visual form.

In the MBLE course the question of purpose is approached in a simple way: during a meditation participants are invited to imagine that they are sitting by a well, and the pick up a pebble. "The pebble carries with it a question ... and when you are ready, dropping the pebble into the water with the question that it carries... "This is my life, I have no other – what do I want to do with it?" Noticing whatever answers splash up and appear in the mind.

THE NEGATIVITY BIAS

MBLE includes discussion of the negativity bias. Although this was not a specific subject of this research, a fascinating discovery from the interviews was how widespread this negativity is, and how it affects the values being considered. Joy is a good example, being either underplayed or even rejected. The need to emphasise the positive comes up here as with psychology - almost as though the Positive Psychology movement needs to be replicated in spirituality[57].

---

[57] This negativity bias has also affected the way Buddhism is seen in the West. As Swearer argues: "The Western scholars and travellers who took up the study of Buddhism in the late 19th and early 20th centuries were enthralled by this story of the Buddha's renunciation and enlightenment. ... It is largely because of these earlier writers, especially Weber, that the West has acquired a skewed portrait of Buddhism as a world-denying religion" (1997). Contrast this with the title of the book by French scientist turned Tibetan Buddhist monk, Matthieu Ricard: Happiness, A Guide To Developing Life's Most Important Skill (2007), or the Dalai Lama's comment "I believe that the very purpose of our life is to seek happiness" (1999:3).

The Negativity Bias

The bit that often gets forgotten in the Christian tradition is Jesus's teaching to love your neighbour as yourself. And those last two words are often are dropped off so Christians can be notoriously bad and some of the negativity and some of the guilt that is carried around by Christians can be linked back to missing those final two words, because if we're not looking after ourselves and caring for ourselves and loving ourselves as well as a neighbour then we don't have the resources.

Christianity is not very good on achievements. And there is this almost insidious pressure to see rejoicing in your achievements, wellbeing and so on as linked to this terrible sin of pride. And again it is a distortion. You can be proud of an achievement, or you can act in a proud and haughty manner that is false and not true to who you are. But if you accomplish some achievement, it is almost as if there is a pressure not to acknowledge anything as good because there is this danger of being seen as pride. And again it comes back to this pressure that has been around within Christianity sometimes that it is all about sacrifice and pain and suffering and costs and so on, and in a sense you can trace that back to the understanding of the passion and crucifixion of Jesus. The theology of suffering for the sins of the world. So you can see where it traces back to, but it has at times gone off in unhelpful directions and that is the cause of Christians carrying a lot of unnecessary guilt with all the ensuing ramifications of that.

Empathetic Joy is not something that's been addressed by Judaism as far as I know. And equanimity is not explicitly addressed.

INTERRELATIONSHIPS

Bentz and Shapiro argue that "The hermeneutic approach assumes the interconnectedness of all aspects and elements of the intersubjective world" (1998, p.112), and this came through strongly in the interviews. Interrelationships emerged in several ways, of which four are selected here.

THE PART AND THE WHOLE

While the research questions focused on individual aspects of the MBLE course, participants saw it as a whole, and all respondents saw relationships between the various values and practices. While individual quotes illustrate this theme, it comes through strongest when looking at interviews as a whole. The different themes and values interlink in people's minds, and they link also to their overall value system. Thus for one respondent Sincerity was a linking theme, for another Mindful Movement, for a third Love.

The Part and the Whole
Bahaullah has said that truthfulness is the foundation of all human virtues so the virtues that you have mentioned are all divine virtues but every virtue that we exercise in life, if it is not based on truth, if it is not based on sincerity, because truthfulness also means to be sincere.
I couldn't separate gratitude, forgiveness, hope. I just think that they are all part of developing healthy constructive loving relationships with people, and for all beings, and everything is interconnected and again we have this thing of saying to be examples and to walk cheerfully over the world and let your life speak.
I do feel that loving-kindness and compassion, equanimity and empathetic joy are all connected, and I feel that if we have been able to be loving and kind to ourselves then we find it easier to be like that with others.

MIND AND BODY

The link between mind and body was readily identified by respondents. For some Mindful Movement has become their primary practice of formal mindfulness.

Mind and Body
When I'm on my prayer mat there is a physical sensation in my heart when I am praying and this is a cultivation of humility. And this is humility and a sense where your mind and heart are aligned.
When I get on my exercise bike, I close my eyes and get into a different state. I am in the moment, and there are 45 minutes when I am just in that moment, I don't know if that is truly a mindful state but I am aware that there are certain periods when I am doing it that I can be in quite a sort of focused spiritual sense. And a sense of spirituality comes in that so that is quite a good thing when it happens.
I think they are very closely linked. I think what we think about and emotions and all that does have an effect on our physical body is, I believe that. You know things like stress and difficulties to have a physical aspect, so I think they are very closely linked and I think we have to take care of both the mind and the body.
There is a lesser commandment to look after your mind and body.
The body can dominate the mind so for example illnesses can take over the mind. It ought to be that the mind helps the body to achieve physical activities and I think that's my preferred view about it, but also the mind can take over and I think that's when bad things happen, when the mind dominates and you forget about the body, and so it's a close relationship between the two and one shouldn't dominate the other. They should link together to create your overall wellbeing.
I do a lot of classes, yoga classes, dance classes, I do those most days and if you're not concentrating in those it's very obvious that you haven't been mindful while you are doing the classes. You go wrong or collide with somebody.

> They are very connected, people see mind and body as being connected
> because when we are trying to get into that space inside us then we are
> listening to what our bodies are saying and we are also connected to each
> other so I don't think you can separate them.

SELF AND OTHERS

When Buddhaghosa detailed the practice of the Four Immeasurables in the
5th century CE he emphasized that "First of all it should be developed only
towards oneself" (1956, p.292), and then gradually extended to embrace an
ever wider circle of beings, and ultimately all sentient beings. This relationship
between self and other is recognised by respondents.

Self and Others
If you can apply (loving-kindness) to yourself you can apply it to others, but it is an essential thing that you have to love and be kind to yourself first.
If you are really being present to yourself and the other then it comes and in Quakerism we are trying to do that in our own meetings both locally and globally, trying to extend it outwards from ourselves to others and then outwards.

COMPLEMENTARITY

The interviews demonstrated that people had no problem in linking the key
themes of MBLE, including meditation and mindfulness, to their existing
belief systems. Several participants also commented on the importance of
community in their tradition, and the creation of an (albeit temporary)
community of practice is an important objective in MBLE.

Complementarity
Mindfulness means to me first of all to have God in the back of your mind all the time, but when you have that it also means that you remember the godly, the divine virtues that God has and at the same time we believe that he has also given all of his attributes, all of his virtues, are within us. Meditation means to me that you actually keep some time in your daily life to sit somewhere quiet and ponder and either use some writings or just your own thoughts … some communication with your soul or God.
Within the Christian tradition there is Brother Lawrence who lived in the 17th century, he was a Carmelite monk, and he wrote a book called 'The Practice of the Presence of God'. He worked in a monastery and his job really was peeling the potatoes, he wasn't regarded as a particularly bright man, as he wasn't working in the scriptorium or anything like that. His job was in the kitchen, and he struggled for a long time with that, trying to figure out where and how God was calling him, and over a period of time he came to the realisation that God was discoverable there in the present, so in peeling the potatoes, in having his hands up to his elbows in potato water and so on, in that moment was the point of encounter and the point of meeting with the divine. In terms of mindfulness within my own tradition I think it is about being attentive to the now because now is the potential point of encounter with the divine.
A big part of our tradition is the community aspect, we are all in it together and our faith has an effect on other people, and sometimes when you know if you are going through a hard time or your faith dwindling and you're wondering what it is all about, the faith of other people or the optimism or the hope, their compassion can carry you along through your hard times until things are better and then you can be helping other people.

Orthodox Jews pray and analyse the texts. And that has to be done in a mindful way and I suppose you could class it as a form of meditation.

Mindfulness for me is being aware of what is happening to me internally on a bodily level, a feeling level, thinking, spirit, soul as well as externally. So it's being present to the present moment. In meeting for worship each person is tuning in or attending to what is happening inwardly as well as outwardly within the gathered group. So we are not just individuals, we are attending to the joint communion within the group. I think that's what we are trying to do it in Quakerism, we wouldn't say that particularly, but I think we are using mindfulness and meditation as the process to tune in to the space, that deeper space within us.

THE BUDDHIST BACKGROUND

Given my concern that Mindfulness Based Life Enhancement should be a secular course open to all, I was interested to know whether my Buddhist background was a problem for participants. Nobody found this to be the case.

Was my Buddhist background an impediment?
No - you couldn't have done it without it.
Not at all, I think it was a help actually, because the fact that you had practiced this for 20 years or so makes you a master of doing this and these presumably came from the Buddhist, and I think that was a brilliant way of taking this beyond just the deep breathing exercises, it gave it much more substance and quality, so I think that was brilliant.
It was very good - it was new to me and I really liked it. I liked it and appreciated it just the way it was.
Not at all - I thought it was very helpful. To me without knowing a whole lot about it Buddhism is more of an embracing philosophy, it embraces equally all different traditions, so it's non-partisan in that sense.

But also I thought that because you are Buddhist your background helps you to be passionate or to convey passion about what you were teaching but also your experience of meditation and mindfulness, you were like a role model in that sense. I think you can't really teach something like that unless you are well versed in it yourself, so basically the fact that you are Buddhist and that you follow this tradition and have followed the tradition where you practice mindfulness meditation and the positive psychology and those Four Immeasurables, you are able to teach them in a very committed way, a very passionate way and I think for others as well certainly I kind of felt when you talked about it or when reading about it in the materials I didn't feel it was just words or just something we have to do in the class. It came across as your way of life and that made it more encouraging to us to want to follow it.

Not at all. In fact I'm not even sure I would have known you were a Buddhist if I hadn't known before.

No not at all, I mean I like Buddhism and I feel that Quakerism and Buddhism are very similar ways of living and I am familiar with, I have read Buddhist books, not loads of them but I have read the popular ones, Lama Surya Das and Pema Chodron, I like her a lot, and years ago I read Alan Watts.

CONCLUSIONS AND IMPLICATIONS

Returning to the purpose of this chapter:

- The Four Immeasurables are explicitly or implicitly expressed in many religions, and are also readily identifiable both those without religious conviction.
- I have identified improvements to the presentation of the Four Immeasurables, in particular for Joy and Equanimity, modifying the language used.
- No problem was expressed by interviewees regarding the origin of the Four Immeasurables or my spiritual tradition.

- The themes of Positive Psychology resonate strongly with participants and interact well the Four Immeasurables. The major modification implied here is the addition of a specific meditation on Self Forgiveness.

First, inquiry into the Four Immeasurables revealed implicit understanding of the terms, in particular Empathetic Joy and Equanimity - even when they are not explicitly clear. This reinforces the assumption that the values should be 'unfolded' to people as already present in them, and the interviews have also identified improved ways of expressing and introducing these values. Recognising the link with Nonaka and Takeuchi's (1995) Knowledge Conversion model, which I have often used in management teaching, proved helpful.

Second, I saw the power of the Negativity Bias, and the way it permeates not only how people think, but their values, beliefs and assumptions too. Third, the interrelationships between qualities emerged strongly. As I have shown in Chapter Three, it is argued in the Buddhist literature on the Four Immeasurables that they mutually reinforce each other: what is encouraging in this research is that respondents referred to such links, and also to links with qualities from Positive Psychology, and with Mindfulness.

Fourth, linked to the above, people readily identified 'the whole' - the MBLE course is experienced as an integrated set of ideas, concepts and practices. When I developed MBLE I brought together four sets of ideas and practices, closely related but from different sources - conventional Mindfulness Based Interventions, Mindful Learning, the Four Immeasurables and Positive Psychology. These were integrated into the overall programme, but for the interviews it was necessary to disaggregate and ask separate questions on each element. As the interviews progressed it became apparent that people saw them as interrelated - in effect they reintegrated them - and those who have been on the course spoke of it as a whole, not the sum of parts. This was a welcome finding, corroborating the intention of the course.

CONTINUATION

Segal et al comment that *"The end of the MBCT program comes too quickly for some patients, and instructors are often faced with requests for follow-up groups or meetings"* (2013:33). And Cullen comments: "Most people benefit dramatically from these programs and want to continue" (2011:191). The same has happened with MBLE: a comment frequently made by participants in the final discussion was that they would like further support to maintain their practice[58], and there are now monthly two-hour Continuation sessions, involving guided meditations, mindful movement and discussion. The first two were general in nature, but I then began more focussed sessions. Thus there have been sessions on Developing Self-Compassion; Cultivating Emotional Balance; Awakening Joy; Buddhist Practice; and each of the Four Immeasurables.

It is interesting to note that the Four Immeasurables feature particularly highly in their minds. I held a one-day session specifically on these, inviting people who had been on the first four courses. 16 people attended, and the feedback was very positive. And when I asked for suggestions for themes for the Continuation sessions, the overwhelming favourite was the Four Immeasurables.

---

[58] For example one person commented on the evaluation questionnaire: "It would be nice to arrange a reunion of the group for a couple of hours to have them talk and feedback about the extent to which they had incorporated the practice into their lives, or not, as the case may be".

8. MINDFULNESS AND LIFE ENHANCEMENT FOR THE SENIOR CITIZEN: POSITIVE AGEING

> In this chapter we consider a specific example of the role that Mindfulness Based Life Enhancement can play in society. The number of senior citizens is increasing all the time – what can MBLE offer us? [declaring an interest here!]

INTRODUCTION

When Levy et al (2002) explored the results of a community-based survey in Ohio, in which 660 individuals aged 50 and older had participated, they found that those with more positive self-perceptions of ageing, measured up to 23 years earlier, lived 7.5 years longer than those with less positive self-perceptions of aging. This in itself makes it worth taking hope and optimism seriously! But seniority is not just about quantity – can mindful life enhancement also provide a greater quality of life for seniors?

More people than ever before find themselves in the 'third age' - and more than ever before are headed here. It can be a time of restriction, withdrawal and negativity. It can alternatively be a time of life enhancement, and mindfulness; the Four Immeasurables and Positive Psychology all have a significant potential role to play here.

Richmond (2012) identifies four stages of ageing:

- *Lightning Strikes* - the moment we truly wake up to our aging, which could be at any time of our lives
- *Coming to Terms* - comparing ourselves now to how we once were
- *Adaptation* - letting go of who we were and embracing who we are
- *Appreciation* - acknowledging that "This is my life, I have no other".

This is therefore a time of reappraisal. Thriving in the third age requires adaptability: *"We must be able to adapt to changing situations, retain confidence in our own resources, accept our limits with good humour, learn how to refuse what we don't want to do, and ensure that our daily routine incorporates time devoted to doing what we enjoy, in peace"* (de Hennezel 2011:135).

It is a time for new approaches to joy and savouring: *"Human life is not condemned to suffering, but destined for joy, happiness, and serenity. The present must be lived for itself; a rich, fulfilled now. In order to rejoice in the present moment, the elderly subject must 'rediscover his ability to enchanted and amazed. If converted to life, old age can successfully turn the present moment into a delight', by opening the individual up to enchantment"* (Misrahi quoted in de Hennezel 2011:171).

It is a time to enhance our relationship with the past: *"It is a fact that anything left in suspense from our past, such as repressed emotions and unresolved conflicts, hinders our development. If we do not become reconciled to our past, we may find ourselves joining the ever-swelling ranks of those who end their lives with dementia"* (ibid:154).

And it is a time for enhancement of the present, and of the mind-body relationship: *"Perhaps more than ever, the skin becomes a place of exchange and of pleasure. The present acquires a new value in which the sensations, thoughts, and emotions of the moment are more fully savoured. There is pleasure in feeling motionless, in existing"* (Pelissier quoted in de Hennezel 2011:212).

WHY LIFE ENHANCEMENT FOR THE SENIOR CITIZEN IS IMPORTANT

In 2012 there were 14.2 million people in the United Kingdom aged 60 and over. The Office for National Statistics has projected that by 2030, compared to 2010, there will be 51% more people aged 65 and over, and 101% more people aged 85 and over (House of Lord 2013:19). ONS project that by 2033 there will be 20.5 million aged 60 and over, out of a total population of 71.6 million[59]. This is part of a world-wide development: the World Health Organization points out that "the number of people aged 65 or older is projected to grow from an estimated 524 million in 2010 to nearly 1.5 billion in 2050, with most of the increase in developing countries" (2011:2). Yet research on MBIs often does not consider their use with seniors. As Smith et al (2007) point out, the primary trial cited in Segal et al (2002), as well as the replication study (Ma & Teasdale 2004), excluded the elderly. In both studies, one of the four inclusion criteria was that participants were aged 18-65 (Teasdale et al 2000:617).

This is important, not only because of the numbers involved, but also because depression is a serious issue for many, affecting 1-in-5 older people living in the community – 2.7 million - and 2-in-5 living in care homes[60]. Smith (2006) argues that mindfulness training should be available to seniors, being relevant to depression, anxiety, physical health and potentially other clinical problems. But if we consider the benefits of mindfulness identified by the Mental Health Foundation (2010) – less psychological distress and depression, less rumination, less negative thoughts, reduced blood pressure, fewer hospital admissions, reduced addictive behaviour, greater empathy, lower social anxiety, more satisfying relationships, more self-compassion - then we can see that all relate as much to seniors as to any other age group. It is a practice which can both address these limiting factors, and enhance the quality of later life.

---

[59] Source: Office for National Statistics. Data available at http://www.ons.gov.uk/ons/index.html
[60] Mental Health Foundation (2010) http://www.mentalhealth.org.uk/information/mental-health-overview/statistics/

LIFE ENHANCEMENT AND THE SENIOR CITIZEN

Although seniors are under-represented or even excluded in much MBI research, there are exceptions. Smith et al (2007) describe results of three courses for older people involving 38 participants, using MBCT with minor modifications. They conclude that most participants found the course beneficial, with 14 of 29 completing the course saying it had been extremely useful, and only one saying it was of no help. The researchers answer the question "Can older people use this approach?" with "Yes. Definitely". McBee (2003) provided MBSR programmes in nursing homes both for residents and for caregivers, and has run a five week telephone class for the homebound elderly, reporting positive results.

Splevins et al, using a MBCT intervention involving 22 predominantly older adults, "found that depression, anxiety and stress levels all decreased" (2009:332), while the ability to be mindful increased significantly. Konnert et al undertook a clinical trial of CBT with nursing home residents. While not an MBI, it included elements of MBCT such as the relationship between thoughts and mood, identifying and scheduling pleasant events, and planning for stressful events. They concluded such an intervention "is beneficial for residents with subsyndromal depression" (2009:295), and point also to a Dutch course, containing many of the same components, which has been "successful with older adults who reside in the community and in nursing homes" (ibid.).

CHALLENGES OF AGEING

Turner (2010) identified five challenges of ageing, and it is worth considering how MBIs may be relevant to each.

HEALTH CONDITIONS

The value of mindful movement to seniors has been identified in research. Tsang and colleagues found that seniors receiving 12 weeks regular qigong exercise "experienced lesser perceived limitations and had a higher sense of mastery and self-efficacy". Research projects exploring MBIs with seniors have reported the need for minor variations only in the movement practices. Smith and colleagues made some modifications following "recommendations by a physiotherapist", designed to minimise risk. As Smith and colleagues (2007:347) comment mindful movement gives people the opportunity to learn more about their bodies, and to discover they are suppler than they may have thought. It also gives the opportunity for positive acceptance of limitations.

Young and Baime argued that "mindfulness training may help seniors successfully manage the physical and psychological challenges of aging in a manner that reduces distress and promotes vitality". They looked at 141 people aged 60 and over who had completed the MBSR programme, and concluded that "overall emotional distress and all sub-scale measurement improved significantly" (2010:59).

Morone, Greco and Weiner reviewed eight mind-body interventions for seniors with persistent pain. These included MBSR, but again they were limited in their findings by the lack of studies looking at seniors. They make some positive comments, in particular on the relevance of yoga, but conclude there is a need for further research. In a subsequent study they provided a MBSR programme to community-dwelling older adults with CLBP, not including yoga or a full-day retreat. They report "sustained benefit from the program as measured by continued meditation by program participants and sustained improvement in physical function and pain acceptance" (2008:316), and comment on the value participants found in an acceptance-based approach to their pain, contrasted to avoidance or control techniques.

LIVING SITUATIONS

According to Help the Aged, loneliness is endemic among pensioners[61]. Creswell et al (2012) undertook a randomised study involving 40 healthy adults aged 55-85, and found that MBSR training reduced loneliness. We can also

---

[61] Reported in The Guardian 20 May 2008 http://www.guardian.co.uk/society/2008/may/20/longtermcare.socialcare

point to a 'side effect' in reported research: McBee comments that "participants often cited the shared group experience as the most beneficial intervention" and even in her telephone based course, there was "an increased awareness of our interconnectedness" (2009:261-2).

Santorelli (1999) describes the whole eight-week programme, including days between each class, as "actualizing the spirit of sangha" (the community) (1999:48). MBI courses for seniors could enhance this aspect, encouraging the creation of a "community of practice and mutual support" which could persist beyond the course. Research shows that formal social activities can be as helpful to well-being as informal activities with friends and neighbours (Okun and colleagues 1984). The positive relationship between social activity and well-being is particularly important in later life (Harlow and Cantor 1996). The growing use of home computers amongst seniors points to further possible enhancements of McBee's (2003) telephone-based mindfulness course.

It has also been argued that mindfulness is relevant to assisted living communities: "while assisted living communities emphasize physical activities for their residents, physical activities can become difficult, even painful, during the aging process. In those cases where exercise is difficult or not possible in an assisted living environment, mindfulness training exercises may be a great alternative to physical exercise in terms of reducing stress."[62]

The home practices involved in an MBI, if continued after the course, can be beneficial in addressing another problem many seniors experience. After a lifetime of work they suddenly find themselves in a much less structured living situation. The Victoria State government in their advice to people retiring says "Daily routine and activities add purpose to life. If there is nothing in particular to do or look forward to on any given day, a person is more likely to feel bored and depressed than a person who lives an active meaningful life."[63] Mindfulness activities address this well.

---

[62] http://www.ambercourtal.com/mindfulness

[63] http://www.betterhealth.vic.gov.au/bhcv2/bhcarticles.nsf/pages/Retirement_issues_to_consider?OpenDocument (2012)

POVERTY

Help the Aged report that 2.2 million UK pensioners are living in poverty, and 25% of seniors are so worried about the future that it is making them ill[64]. MBIs cannot address poverty, but they could help address this worry. While many seniors are physically resource-poor, there are other areas in which they are resource-rich, notably time. Smith comments that many seniors have more free time which could mean that attention is given to the task in hand, rather than being divided [quoted in Splevins et al, 2009]. The latter also suggest that "the ability to observe and to act with awareness may be skills which naturally increase with age" (2009:332).

As Kabat-Zinn says, mindfulness can involve "dwelling inwardly for extended periods", through which "we come to know something of the poverty of always looking outside ourselves for happiness, understanding and wisdom" (1994:96). MBIs offer seniors the opportunity to reflect on, and perhaps recast, their perceptions of poverty. Mindfulness also requires little material wealth.

MENTAL HEALTH

MBCT has achieved long-term reduction in depression in older people (Smith 2006), while DBT has helped chronically depressed older adults (Lynch and Bronner 2006). Two studies of older African Americans and Native Hawaiians suggest that Transcendental Meditation may be an effective approach to reducing depression (Medical News Today 2010). There is also evidence that CBT is beneficial to seniors with depression. Laidlaw and colleagues argue that "in our experience, CBT is effective, adaptable and very popular with older people" (2003:xi).

More generally, mindfulness can help mental balance: "Particularly relevant for older adults is the concept of conative balance, in short, re-evaluating priorities and making certain that their daily behaviour is consistent with how they want to be remembered" (Rejeski 2008:140).

---

[64] Reported in The Guardian (see footnote above)

Ageism is pervasive in modern society (Darwin et al 1979). Stereotyping of the elderly is well summarised in Age Concern's publication on ageism (2004). One of their branches discovered participants on a computing skills course were being turned away from a local computer store because the young staff "assumed that because of the customer's age they would not be able to deal with the 'complexities' of buying a computer" (2004:11).

De Hennezel quotes de Ladoucette: "People are afraid of growing old because they cannot bear the way other people will see them. Old people are made to feel that they are an ugly, useless burden on society" (2011:58). Langer argues that "Stereotypes regarding the negative consequences of old age are widely known and are almost unconditionally accepted, at least in the West. Studies have shown that old people are seen as forgetful, slow, weak, timid, and set in their ways" (2009:153-4).

Kite et al (1991) surveyed research, concluding "Characteristics associated with older individuals are not well defined, but there is general agreement that the stereotype is multidimensional and includes characteristics such as ill, tired, grouchy, unlikely to participate in activities, unhappy, undesirable for company, and physically unattractive" (1991:20). More recently, Cuddy et al (2005) argue that seniors are stereotyped as low on competence. A brief survey of internet articles adds: they are bad drivers, set in their ways, all have Alzheimers, are mean and crotchety, smell like old milk, or mothballs, can't remember important things. Cuddy et al conclude that "exposure to stereotype-inconsistent and individuating information could help to undo the elderly stereotype by restoring a sense of esteem for older people" (2005:280).

Particularly relevant here is self-stereotyping, including learned helplessness. O'Brien Cousins (2000) surveyed 143 women aged 70+ about their beliefs regarding six fitness activities, including slow stretching. She found their beliefs about risks were strong and sometimes sensational. A good proportion could not see the relevance of exercises making their bodies stretch and bend. She suggests "Older women may have adopted an attitude of learned helplessness because many of them simply lack the confidence and personal resources to participate in active recreation" (2000:290). In addition to challenging this learned helplessness, mindful movement could provide a wider context for seniors to see the relevance of these exercises, while the bodyscan could help them explore further the sensational aspects of their concerns.

Langer comments that "older adults often hold negative feelings about the elderly that are as strong, if not stronger, than those held by younger adults" (2009:154). Levy (2001) argues "research suggests that after a lifetime of exposure to a culture's age stereotypes, older individuals direct these age stereotypes inwards" (2001:579). She draws on the finding of a number of researchers to conclude that "As individuals age, these stereotypes tend to be reinforced by repeated exposure to the mainly negative aging stereotypes that exist in North America and Europe" (2003:203). Moreover, these self-stereotypes "can operate without awareness to influence cognitive and physical outcomes" (ibid:2008). However, both positive and negative ageing self-stereotypes can be activated, and with colleagues she has undertaken research which found that seniors with more positive self-perceptions of aging lived over seven years longer than those with less positive self-perceptions. They conclude that this can in part be addressed by "encouraging older individuals to monitor the correspondence between the ways they are targeted by others and the ways they target themselves" (Levy et al 2002), leading to "ways you can see your thoughts differently" (Segal et al 2013:323). Here the dynamic between acceptance and resignation is important: as they point out, acceptance requires conscious commitment and energy, whereas resignation "implies passivity and a degree of helplessness" (2002:221).

MINDFULNESS AND LIFE ENHANCEMENT IN THE THIRD AGE

In recent years there have been many reports on healthy living, some general, some more specifically relating to the senior. Here we review a sample and demonstrate the relevance of mindfulness and life enhancement.

The New Economics Foundation (2008) has identified five ways to wellbeing: Connect, Be Active, Take Notice, Give and Keep Learning. All five can be addressed in mindfulness programmes. As we have seen, MBLE includes mindful movement (Be Active), meditation (Take Notice) and Gratitude and Kindness (Give). It explores a variety of approaches which can help the individual (Keep Learning), and is done in a group setting which encourages discussion and new links (Connect). The Foundation's report concludes *"a wellbeing approach to education might consider how to integrate the promotion of emotional and social wellbeing into the ethos of schools. The Five Ways to Wellbeing could be directly applied to thinking about a broader curriculum that provides more opportunities around sports, arts, creativity and mindfulness in lessons"* (2008:28-9).

The Executive Summary of the report Fair Society, Healthy Lives (The Marmot Review) concludes *"Services that promote the health, well-being and independence of older people and, in so doing, prevent or delay the need for more intensive or institutional care, make a significant contribution to ameliorating health inequalities"* (2010:14). The report by the Department of Health 'Healthy Lives, Healthy People' states *"We will make active ageing the norm rather than the exception"* (2010:7).

The House of Lords Select Committee argue that there need to be *"radical changes in the way that health and social care serve the population"* (2013:11), and that *"many of our growing older population are in good health, will retire with a decent income and a strong social network, have much to offer society, and will want to combine work with new activities, volunteering and caring"* (2013:27). One of the changes needs to be greater emphasis on ways by which seniors can maintain this good health, and mindfulness has role to play here.

Finally, in their report on "The role of local government in promoting wellbeing", the Local Government Improvement And Development and The National Mental Health Development Unit conclude: *"People's sense of how their lives are going, and the strength of relationships that sustain community life, are strongly influenced by psychological and social wellbeing: Having a positive outlook in life and feeling good about oneself the elements that make up emotional wellbeing directly promote a more positive experience of life. Resilience - the ability of individuals or communities to cope positively with change, challenge, adversity and shock - can reduce the impact of risk factors in the external environment, such as the recent recession. Feeling connected to others, feeling in control, feeling capable, and having a sense of purpose all contribute to enabling a person to flourish"* (2010:11).

None of these reports refer to mindfulness – an indication of the need to continue putting this argument forcibly.

CONCLUSION

Walsh argues that "health professionals have significantly underestimated the importance of lifestyle for mental health … considerable research and clinical evidence support the following eight Therapeutic Lifestyle Changes: exercise, nutrition and diet, time in nature, relationships, recreation, relaxation and stress management, religious and spiritual involvement, and contribution and service to others" (2011:579-580). MBLE incorporates exercise (mindful movement), nutrition (mindful eating), time in nature (mindful walking), recreation and enjoyable activities (savouring), stress management (meditation), and contribution and service to others (for example through the Four Immeasurables). It is designed to be compatible with religious and spiritual involvement, encouraging exploration of values and purpose, and when done as a course it embraces the specific objective of developing relationships between participants through a 'community of practice'. The Four Immeasurables, and practices such as tonglen, emphasise relationships and the interconnection between us all.

Mindfulness and positive psychology have important contributions to make to a Strategy for an Ageing Population. Physical and mental wellbeing are key to life enhancement at any age, and it is never too late to begin such activities (and here I speak from personal experience – while I have meditated for many years, and done Pilates for over a decade, I began yoga aged 61 – and now attend five classes a week). Rejeski comments that "A mindfulness perspective can benefit the promotion of physical activities and a new relationship with the body in aging. Likewise, physical activities in the context of aging provide an ideal means of developing mindfulness in day-to-day life" (2008:139). The practices which constitute MBLE, and which are brought together in the next chapter, therefore have much to offer the senior citizen.

And it can be taken further. De Hennezel gives many examples of the differing perspectives people have of ageing, and concludes "Everything depends upon the way we look at life" (2011:95). It is again the contrast between an optimistic and a pessimistic approach, and also between Being and Doing, as in the following example she gives: "The important thing is no longer to run to do something but to stop and dream, look at the sky, chat with the person next to you" (ibid:94). And this can involve a mental 'spring-clean' of "the sorrows which had to be liberated, the forgiveness she needed to grant herself" (ibid).

Richmond proposes that "Aging is an ideal time for the cultivation of the inner life: a time for spiritual practice" (2012:13). In his book he identifies a number of practices which the senior (or indeed anyone) can add to MBLE. There is the Gratitude Walk, mindful walking in which you appreciate and express gratitude for all around you. There is the Meditation on Horizontal and Vertical Time, distinguishing horizontal time – from birth to maturity and beyond – from vertical time "Which means this present moment: this room, this body, this breath. While horizontal time is largely mental, vertical time is more physical and is expressed in the body and breath" (2012:78). There is Contemplative Reflection, which "focuses on identity – the way we lose old pieces of our identity as we age, and the opportunity to create new identities to replace what we have lost" (2012:187). And there is the Day Away – in effect, a Day of Practice which can be undertaken on one's own. It may be a full day, or a half day, and it can draw on the many guided practices now available, including mindful movement and mindful walking.

Shunryu Suzuki was once asked "Why do we meditate?" He answered, "So you can enjoy your old age" (Richmond 2012:6). There is no better conclusion to this chapter!

9 . MINDFULNESS BASED LIFE ENHANCEMENT

In this chapter we integrate the themes explored throughout this book, exploring the daily practice of MBLE through eight interlinked themes.

Mindfulness Based Life Enhancement was conceived as an integration of mindfulness, mindful learning, the Four Immeasurables and Positive Psychology. As we have seen, participants do experience it as an integrated approach, which contributes to their way of living, and a helpful way of seeing this emerged from the Reflective Experiential Action Learning discussions held in the final week of each course. We saw that MBLE comes together for participants as having eight interlinked themes: these are a reflection of what people have said, and what they have learnt.

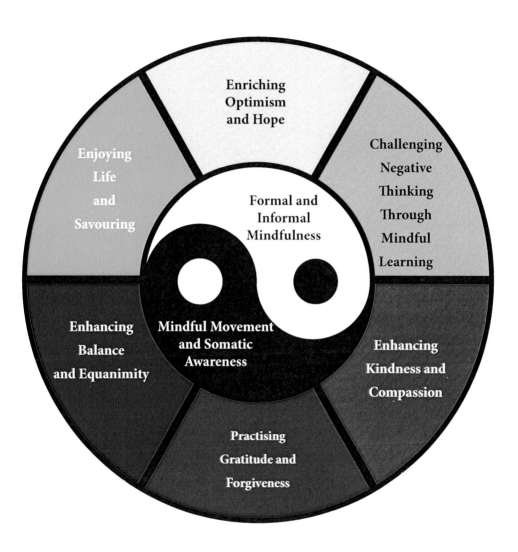

Figure 9-1: MINDFULNESS-BASED LIFE ENHANCEMENT

At the heart of MBLE is practice - Mindfulness and Mindful Movement - developing mindfulness of mind, body, feelings and experiences. Surrounding these are six themes which have come up time and again, and it is therefore useful to expand on each of these to illustrate Mindfulness Based Life Enhancement as on ongoing practice. Just as the Four Immeasurables mutually support each other, and just as Positive Emotions 'broaden and build' [Frederickson], so these eight aspects of MBLE interrelate and reinforce each other, forming a "pattern that connects" (Bateson 1973). You may wish to explore how this Pattern works best for you. The advice is to practice the White and Black Links every day. In addition, you may wish to focus each day on one of the other six Links – or to focus on one for several days. The choice is yours!

If you wish to practice MBLE, there are a number of guided meditations which are available at the website http://mindfulenhance.org/. These include the Core Recordings, including the Four Immeasurables, which are used during the eight week programme. These can be used to enhance the eight links discussed in Chapter Ten. There are also a series of shorter guided meditations, ranging from 5 to 15 minutes, which are primarily intended for use, when you are short of time.

You will also find at the website additional resources relating to Mindfulness Based Life Enhancement, including an outline of the course structure.

THE WHITE LINK: PRACTISING FORMAL AND INFORMAL MINDFULNESS

Not surprisingly, mindfulness – of both mind and body – is at the heart of MBLE. Formal practice develops the 'mental muscle' of mindfulness – the physical analogy is very apt. As Fronsdal and Pandita put it "Much as we might develop physical strength, balance, and stability of the body in a gym, so too can we develop strength, balance and stability of the mind" (2005:45). But it is through informal mindfulness that this comes into everyday life.

- The key here is to engage in formal practice, if possible every day.
- Guided meditations of varying length – from 5 minutes to 30 minutes – are available on the accompanying website.
- Guided meditations are also available on websites and with books on mindfulness and meditation.
- When you are short of time, use the Jewel Programmes [5 to 15 minutes long].
- Practise informal mindfulness, such as washing dishes, listening to others, gardening, sporting activity – the list is endless!
- Maintain Mindful Competence, and develop the Mindful Space which helps Mindful Change.
- Go on a retreat.

How the other links in MBLE can help:

- Challenging negative thinking through mindful learning: maintaining Mindful Competence, the integration of Beginner's Mind and Expert Mind.
- Engaging in Mindful Movement can be an excellent way of enhancing both formal and informal mindfulness. Participants have cited running, cycling, spinning, swimming, walking (especially in parks or countryside). *"I particularly benefit from walking and eating slowly exercise." "Generally incorporate into how I am in daily life. Doing one thing at a time (not always though!)"*

THE ORANGE LINK: CHALLENGING NEGATIVE THINKING THROUGH MINDFUL LEARNING

MBLE explores the negativity bias as a key finding in Positive Psychology, and makes use of findings from psychological research and logic, which have informed both CBT and organisational theory, including examination of the cognitive distortions to which we are frequently subject.

- Keep an open mind, as advocated centuries ago by the Pyrrhonists, can be helpful, as can the principles of mindful learning advocated by Langer: the creation of new categories, openness to new information, and awareness of more than one perspective.
- Challenge negative thinking using the ABCDE sequence:
  - A for Action
  - B for Belief
  - C for Consequence
  - D for Dispute
  - E for Effect or Energisation
- Watch for cognitive distortions, such as overgeneralisation, jumping to conclusions, and catastrophising.
- Learn to argue with yourself, by exploring the evidence, the alternatives, the implications.
- Follow the principles of mindful learning: the creation of new categories, openness to new information, and awareness of more than one perspective.
- The Two Darts metaphor is helpful for many. The first is inevitable: it comes to us and causes pain. The second dart is optional: we fire it at ourselves and it causes suffering, magnifying the effect of the first. So don't fire it!

How the other links in MBLE can help:

- Practising formal and informal mindfulness: *"I find I am more able to stop negative feelings escalating and can use mindfulness to ground me and put things back in perspective".*

- Enriching optimism and hope: recognising the contrast between optimistic and pessimistic viewpoints on particular situations, and choosing where possible to move toward a more optimistic stance.

- Practising gratitude and forgiveness: not beating up on yourself when you get things wrong: practising self-forgiveness.

- Enhancing balance and equanimity: this is not about eliminating negative thoughts, in the way that 'positive thinking' advocates argue. Rather it is about developing a healthy balance between the positive and the negative.

THE RED LINK: ENHANCING KINDNESS AND COMPASSION

Loving-kindness - a genuine feeling of caring and respect for others – and compassion – the wish to alleviate suffering without pity or condescension – are the two most familiar Immeasurables. They support each other. Compassion prevents loving-kindness from forgetting that, while both are enjoying or giving temporary and limited happiness, there still exists much suffering in the world. Loving-kindness guards against partiality, prevents compassion from discrimination by selecting and excluding and thus protects it from falling into partiality or aversion against the excluded side.

PRACTISING THE RED LINK
<ul><li>Use the guided meditations on Loving Kindness, Compassion and the Four Immeasurables.</li><li>Practice tonglen.</li><li>Commit 'Random acts of kindness', whenever and wherever you can.</li><li>Watch for the Near Enemies of kindness and compassion – attachment, greed, pity and grief – and seek to minimise these.</li><li>Watch for the Far Enemies of kindness and compassion – hatred, ill-will and cruelty – and seek to avoid these.</li><li>Practice Mindful Listening.</li><li>When you are under pressure, cultivate self-compassion with the Three Minute Breathing Space, or with RAIN.</li></ul>

RAIN
• **Recognise** when a strong emotion is present. This involves stepping out of denial and acknowledging what is present in our experience.
• **Allow** or acknowledge that it is there. This is acceptance: Instead of trying to judge, explain or manipulate how we feel, we can simply maintain an open presence in the face of it.
• **Investigate** the body, thoughts and emotions. In doing this we cultivate a quality of curiosity and interest
• **Non-identify** with whatever is there. Inquire of every mental state or emotion that arises – is this really who I am or is this just an experience that is moving through me?

How the other links in MBLE can help:

- Practising formal and informal mindfulness: there are many guided meditations in loving kindness and meditation available.
- Enjoying life and savouring[65]: Empathetic Joy helps to recognise that it is not all suffering and grief, and that we can attend also to the joys and virtues of ourselves and other. And it holds compassion back from becoming overwhelmed by the sight of the world's suffering, from being absorbed by it to the exclusion of everything else.
- Enhancing balance and equanimity: Equanimity guards compassion from being dissipated and from going astray in uncontrolled emotion. It helps develop composure and internal calm allowing one to know what can or cannot be done.

---

[65] Here and in the following sections we draw on the linkages identified by Wallace, McLeod and Nyanaponika Thera discussed in Chapter 3.

Gratitude and forgiveness are important values and practices. Directed toward the self, they enhance positive feelings about life. Directed toward others, they express interconnection. Like other themes in MBLE, the issue is not persuading people to adopt them. But an explicit focus leads to new insights, and enhancement of their role.

Each is therefore important in its own right, but why consider them together? First, "gratitude and forgiveness are theoretically linked character strengths" which "share a common, fundamental component of empathy" (Breen et al 2010:932-3). From a study of 140 participants they conclude that "People who reported greater levels of gratitude and forgiveness also tended to report less anger and subjective feelings of loneliness as well as fewer depressive symptoms. These same people also reported greater acceptance, empathy and self-compassion" (ibid::935). Neto's study of 152 participants concluded that "gratitude explained a significant amount of variance of overall propensity to forgive" (2007:2313). He quotes Vaillant's (1993) argument that "a key to mature adaptation to life is the ability to replace bitterness and resentment toward those who have perpetrated harm with gratitude and acceptance" (ibid:2321).

Second, gratitude can prove a helpful counterbalance to negative thoughts such as lack of forgiveness – one way to deal with disturbing thoughts recommended by the Buddha (see Box 8). For example, if a close friend has done something you find hard to forgive, cultivating a sense of gratitude for their friendship can help in putting this transgression in the wider context of your positive relationship.

- Ritualise gratitude, for example through a gratitude journal, or writing down three things for which you are grateful each evening.
- Write a letter of gratitude to someone, and perhaps delivering it personally.
- Express gratitude for each meal.
- Say 'thank you' often – to yourself, to others.
- Practice self-forgiveness.
- Write a forgiveness letter, which you may or may not deliver.
- Look to the positive aspects of a relationship, and feeling grateful for these, when the other person has caused you harm.
- Think about the eight ways that gratitude can boost happiness (Table 4.3).

How the other links in MBLE can help:

- Challenging negative thinking through mindful learning: "The process of forgiveness involves reconceptualising past offenses with awareness and empathy, which leads to the letting go of blame and replacing it with a kinder, more generous outlook. Anger and resentment are the glue that holds negative beliefs in place, blocking the way to peace and happiness. As such, the interaction of cognitive and spiritual techniques works to undo this maintenance of negativity, replacing it with goodwill and positivity" (Menahem and Love 2013:830).
- Enhancing kindness and compassion: again the comments of Menahem and Love are relevant: "Genuine forgiveness is wholly intrapersonal and involves the injured person choosing to abandon a sense of blame and replacing that feeling with compassion; it is unconditional and does not rely on the offender's response" (2013:829).
- Enhancing Balance and Equanimity: *"When I was on the course I felt a whole lot calmer and better-disposed towards others".*

For hard issues - usually resentments about events that have had a long-term effect - there is great value in the five ways of dealing with the disturbing thoughts that arise during formal meditation.

- Think of something skilful (positive) to help dissolve an unskilful (negative) thought. "In order to dissipate a negative thought you only have to bring up in the mind something positive as a counter-medicine or antidote to it. For example a compassionate thought could replace a hateful one" (Batchelor 2011:161).
- Scrutinize the drawbacks of the unskilful thoughts (RAIN helps here). "Consider carefully the consequences of our thoughts and realise that certain types of thoughts are indeed liable to produce painful results" (Batchelor, 2011:162).
- Pay no attention to the thoughts, abandoning them and allowing them to subside (my experience has been that next time they arise, there is less to confront). "When certain thoughts are simply too strong or disturbing to deal with directly, the best way to dissipate them may be simply to think of something else" (Batchelor, 2011:162).
- Look into the root of the thought (for example, using Backtracking, the Moment of Arising, and the Cycle of Thought (Nairn 1999:69-81).
- Stop them by pure will: "he should beat down, constrain, and crush his mind with his awareness"- very much the action of last resort! But as Batchelor comments, "I like the pragmatism of the Buddha; if everything else fails and you continue to have disturbing and destructive thoughts, then stop them by sheer force of will" (2011:163).

Buddha's Discourse on the Forms of Thought (Vitakkasanthana Sutta), Batchelor 2011.

THE BLUE LINK: ENHANCING BALANCE AND EQUANIMITY

Enhancing equanimity is helped by using the seven characteristics identified by Fronsdal and Pandita (2005:43-5), discussed in Chapter Three: Integrity, Faith, A well-developed mind, Well-being, Understanding or wisdom, Insight, and Freedom. It is the "spaciousness that comes from seeing a bigger picture" (ibid). It is the challenge to, and rejection of, prejudice.

PRACTISING THE BLUE LINK

- Use the guided meditations on Equanimity and the Four Immeasurables.
- Use the Mountain and Lake guided meditations.
- Practice tonglen.
- Watch for the Near Enemies of equanimity – indifference and foolish unknowing – and seeking to minimise these.
- Watch for the Far Enemies of equanimity – greed, partiality, prejudice and discrimination – and seeking to avoid these.
- Practice mindful acceptance.
- Ensure balance between care of self and care of others. Richmond quotes Russell: "The people I see who really do well with the aging are the ones who divide their time between actively helping others and doings things that are just for them, things that give them enjoyment and pleasure. You've got to put something in both baskets – giving to others and giving to yourself. You have to find that balance" (2012:146).

TONGLEN

- As you breathe in, take in the suffering, discomfort and pain of the person or persons you have chosen (which may be yourself). You may visualise this as a dark cloud.
- Pause briefly at the end of the in-breath, and visualise this dark cloud being transformed and purified in your heart.
- Now breathe out your wishes of love, compassion, joy and well-being, perhaps visualising this in the form of bright white light.

How the other links in MBLE can help:

- Practising formal and informal mindfulness: there are a growing number of guided meditations in equanimity available.
- Enhancing kindness and compassion: Loving-kindness addresses indifference and detachment, which is a form of shutting down. It encourages selflessness, and even fervour. For fervour, too, transformed and controlled, is part of perfect equanimity, strengthening its power of keen penetration and wise restraint. Compassion attends to and reminds us of the suffering in the world; it guards equanimity from falling into a cold indifference, and keeps it from indolent or selfish isolation.
- Enjoying life and savouring: Empathetic joy gives to equanimity the mild serenity that softens its stern appearance. It is the smile that persists in spite of our knowledge of the world's suffering, a smile that gives solace and hope, fearlessness and confidence.
- Engaging in Mindful Movement and somatic awareness: there are many balances in yoga and Pilates, and these are an excellent way to become mindful – for the simple reason that if you lose focus, you lose your posture!

THE GREEN LINK: ENJOYING LIFE AND SAVOURING

Life Enhancement comes through here in the twin activities of savouring and practising empathetic joy.

PRACTISING THE GREEN LINK
<ul><li>Use the guided meditations on Empathetic Joy and the Four Immeasurables.</li><li>Practice tonglen.</li><li>Take a savouring vacation – even if it is only five minutes – every day.</li><li>Focus on the ten savouring strategies (Table 4.6), and employ these wherever possible.</li><li>Savour food – eat mindfully.</li><li>Practice the yoga of smiling.</li></ul>

- Watch for the Near Enemies of empathetic joy – joy tinged with insincerity or personal identification; forms of joy that are excessive such as elation, exuberance; Schadenfreude – and seek to minimise these.
- Watch for the Far Enemies of empathetic joy– envy, jealousy, aversion – and seek to avoid these.

How the other links in MBLE can help:

- Practising formal and informal mindfulness: there are a growing number of guided meditations in empathetic joy available.
- Enhancing kindness and compassion: Loving-kindness brings us back to the desire that all beings will find genuine happiness and its causes, avoiding frivolity and hedonism. Compassion prevents empathetic joy from forgetting that, while both are enjoying or giving temporary and limited happiness, there still exists much suffering in the world. Empathetic joy needs understanding and compassion and equanimity if you are to avoid becoming a Pollyanna.
- Enhancing balance and equanimity: Equanimity addresses the dangers of exaggerated elation by encouraging us to notice how we react to whatever arises in experience.

THE YELLOW LINK: ENRICHING OPTIMISM AND HOPE

Although distinct[66], hope and optimism are closely interrelated, and they also provide important linkages to people's wider belief systems, giving them the opportunity to consider purpose and meaning in their lives. Participants in MBLE are encouraged to relate the values to their existing value system, with the focus on enhancing what already exists.

---

[66] Hope is definitely not the same thing as optimism. It is not the conviction that something will turn out well, but the certainty that something makes sense, regardless of how it turns out." – Vaclav Havel

PRACTISING THE YELLOW LINK

- Practice thought experiments which compare optimistic and pessimistic viewpoints.
- Relate mindfulness to your existing belief system, and consider values, purpose and meaning.
- Write a Best Possible Future Diary: This exercise involves considering your most important, deeply held goals and picturing that they will be achieved. Research shows writing about this for 20 minutes occasionally will increase positive moods and well being.
- Consider Goals and Sub goals: To further develop hopeful thinking try breaking your big goals into sub goals and the action plans required to achieve these goals.
- Identify automatic pessimistic thoughts and challenge them.
- Develop realistic optimism.

DEVELOPING REALISTIC OPTIMISM

- Leniency for the Past : the 'Benefit of the Doubt' principle. Select an interpretation of past performances or events which focuses on the positive aspects of the situation.
- Appreciation for the Present: The 'Appreciate the Moment' Principle. Be alert to the positive aspects of the current situation and feel thankful for what you have and for your circumstances.
- Opportunity-seeking for the future: the 'Windows of Opportunity' Principle. When considering future goals and plans depict the situation as a challenge or opportunity rather than as a chore or a problem (Schneider 2001:254-6).

How the other links in MBLE can help:

- Challenging negative thinking through mindful learning: "I'm an optimistic person by nature. But the course has shown me how much negativity there is around (e.g. in academic institutions.) and how easy it is to get caught up in that automatically. So it helps me pull back from the negativity. I'm currently trying to remember to turn negative thoughts and words round into positive ones."

- Enjoying life and savouring: "I have a greater appreciation of the value of noticing someone else experiencing joy and taking time to savour the moment with them and to stay with it. Also, to be aware that if I feel happy, maybe that has a positive effect on others".

- Enhancing balance and equanimity: we are not seeking a Pollyanna state, but rather a healthy balance. Keats advocated the quality of Negative Capability, when one "is capable of being in uncertainties, mysteries, doubts, without any irritable reaching after fact and reason"[67]. And Seligman points to the benefits of mild forms of pessimism, which help in "pulling us back a bit from the risky exaggerations of our optimism, making us think twice, keeping us from making rash, foolhardy gestures" (2006:114).

THE BLACK LINK: ENGAGING IN MINDFUL MOVEMENT AND SOMATIC AWARENESS

We return to the centre of our model for the final link. Popular as mindfulness has become, it has a name which can be misleading, reinforcing the emphasis on the mind which has been a feature of Western thinking for centuries, particularly since Descartes' split between mind and body. The Four Foundations of Mindfulness provide a valuable corrective to this, provided Mindfulness of the Body is not interpreted only as mindfulness about the body – somatic awareness. The emphasis on mindful movement in MBLE has proved popular – leading often to people taking up, or renewing, practice of yoga, TaiChi, ChiGong or other forms of physical activity. And those who are already involved in physical practice have strengthened the mind-body link. A review of research on yoga concluded that "Many studies included in the review reported statistically significant positive outcomes, and this is very encouraging for an intervention as complex and variable as yoga, applied across such a wide range of conditions" (Harnan et al 2013:64).

---

[67] In a letter to his brothers George and Thomas Keats, on 21 December 1817.

This of course contrasts sharply with the alternative view of yoga as purely physical, as espoused by Broga: "It's yoga for dudes – and anyone else who wants the physical benefits of the exercise regime without all the mystical stuff …They come for no-nonsense yoga, with minimal meditating but all of the breathing and positions that make the practice so good for you."[68]

PRACTISING THE BLACK LINK

- Overall, the message here is simple – take every opportunity to practise mindful movement, and do some every day.
- If you have any form of exercise regime, then seek to do it mindfully.
- There are three mindful movements recommended by many yoga and Pilates teachers, and these are worth doing every day. They are cat, the pelvic tilt, and floppy doll.
- Practice mindful walking, sometimes slowly, sometimes at a normal pace.
- You can find many examples of practice in yoga, tai chi and qigong on YouTube – but best of all is to go to a class!
- Do a bodyscan to enhance somatic awareness.

How the other links in MBLE can help:

- Practising formal and informal mindfulness – maintaining a mindful approach to movement, and not letting it turn into mindless activity.
- Challenging negative thinking through mindful learning, for example by recognising the problems that arise when yoga practice becomes competitive, leading to a focus on what you can or cannot do, rather than a mindful approach to the movement.
- Enhancing kindness and compassion to yourself – looking after your body when practising mindful movement and appreciating its scope and its limitations. In addition, a compassionate approach to difficult situations can involve mindfulness of the body: "Notice where the anxiety is held within our body ... notice what kind of sensations we

---

[68] The Busy Man's Guide to Broga Simon Usborne The I 16 July 2013.

are experiencing ... notice if we are resisting these sensations ... Then notice what happens if we open to them with kindness and acceptance" (Gilbert and Choden 2013:227).

- Enjoying life and savouring – enjoy the activity and savour every movement.
- Enhancing balance and equanimity – balance movements are excellent ways to be mindful – loss of focus means you fall out of the balance!
- Practising gratitude and forgiveness – being grateful for what you can do, and forgiving your body for what it finds too difficult.

THE PATTERN THAT CONNECTS

The eight links outlined in this Chapter form a pattern that connects. Participants in MBLE often illustrate how it all comes together for them, reporting:

- Being less fearful and more trusting
- Less angry
- More forgiving
- Less stressed and anxious
- More thoughtful about how they are going to respond to people
- More present
- More able to manage poor health
- More focussed at work.

When I developed MBLE I deliberately chose the term 'Life Enhancement' to emphasise the positive aspects. What has become clear to me, as I have learnt alongside participants, is that 'enhancement' applies much more generally.

- We are already mindful at times; formal mindfulness practices enhance this capability.
- We recognise the problems that automatic pilot, negative thinking and rumination can cause, but may not have explored the full consequences and seen the possibilities of changing our relationship to these.
- We display the qualities of loving kindness, compassion, empathetic joy

and equanimity at times, but all of these can be deepened and enhanced through formal practice.

- We all have our own levels of optimism, hope, gratitude and forgiveness, but these can be extended and enhanced.
- We know how to savour and make the most of the present moment, but often lose sight of its full potential, especially when we get trapped on the hedonic treadmill.
- We understand the importance of the link between mind and body, but this understanding can be easily lost, and can be enhanced through mindful movement.
- We all have existing values and our own worldview; MBLE is compatible with these and helps people enhance what they already have.

The evidence shows that MBLE provides the necessary scaffolding for participating to continue and deepen their practice. These eight interlinked practices can be recommended to all interested in life enhancement through mindfulness. It is to be hoped that this book has helped to explain why this is so.

10. BIBLIOGRAPHY

AGE CONCERN (2004) Ageism Exists Age Concern accessed http://www.seniorsnetwork.co.uk/ageism/acebooklet.pdf

ARGYRIS, C. (1986) Skilled Incompetence Harvard Business Review September

ARMSTRONG, K. (2011) Twelve Steps To A Compassionate Life Bodley Head

ASPINWALL, L. (2005) Happier and Wiser in Snyder, C.R. and Lopez, S.J. (edited) Handbook of Positive Psychology Oxford: Oxford University Press

ASTIN, J. (1997). Stress reduction through mindfulness meditation: Effects on psychological symptomatology, sense of control, and spiritual experience. Psychotherapy and Psychosomatics, 66:97-106

BAER, R., SMITH, G., HOPKINS, J., KRIETEMEYER, J. and TONEY, L (2006) Using Self-Report Assessment Methods to Explore Facets of Mindfulness Assessment Vol 13 No 1 Positive Psychology 27-45

BANDURA, A. (2006) A Murky Portrait of Human Cruelty Behavioral and Brain Sciences 29:3 p 225

BARAZ, J. and ALEXANDER, S. (2010) Awakening Joy New York: Bantam

BARWICK, D. (2000) George's Failed Quest for Happiness: An Aristotelian Analysis in Irwin, W. (ed) Seinfeld and Philosophy Peru: Carus Publishing

BATCHELOR, M. (2011) Meditation and Mindfulness Contemporary Buddhism Vol 12 No 1

BATESON, G. (1973) Steps to an Ecology of Mind St Albans:Granada

BAUMEISTER, R., BRATSLAVSKY, E., FINKENAUER, C. and VOHS, K. (2001) Bad is Stronger than Good Review of General Psychology 5 (4): 323-370. Available at http://dionysus.psych.wisc.edu/Lit/Articles/BaumeisterR2001a.pdf.

BECK, A. T. (1976); Burns, D. D. (1980) Cognitive therapies and emotional disorders New York: New American Library

BENTZ, V. and SHAPIRO, J. (1998) Mindful Inquiry in Social Research London:Sage

BERLINER, D.C. (2001) Learning about and learning from expert teachers International Journal of Educational Research 35-463-482

BIRNIE, K., SPECA, M. and CARLSON, L. (2010) Exploring Self-compassion and Empathy in the Context of Mindfulness-based Stress Reduction Stress and Health 26: 359-371

BLOCK-LERNER, J., ADAIR, C., PLUMB, J.C., RHATIGAN, D.L., & ORSILLO, S.M. (2007). The case for mindfulness-based approaches in the cultivation of empathy: Does nonjudgmental, present-moment awareness increase capacity for perspective-taking and empathic concern? Journal of Marital & Family Therapy, 33(4), 501–516.

BODIFORD, W. (1997) Zen and the Art of Religious Prejudice in Zen Quarterly Vol. 9. Nos. 1 and 2

BOWDEN, M. (2001) Black Hawk Down: A Study Of Modern War New York: Signet

BOYATZIS, R. and MCKEE, A. (2005) Resonant Leadership Boston: Harvard Business School Press

BRACH, T. (2003) Radical Acceptance New York: Bantam Dell

BREEN, W., KASHDA, T., LENSER, M. and FINCHMAN, F. (2010) Gratitude and Forgiveness: Convergence and Divergence on Self-Report And Informant Ratings Personality And Individual Differences 49:932-937

BRYANT, F.B. and VEROFF, J. (2007) Savoring: A new model of Positive experience Mahwah, NJ:Lawrence Erlbaum Associates

BUDDHAGHOSA (1956) Visuddhimagga: The Path of Purification Translated by Bhikkhu Nanamoli Singapore: Buddhist Meditation Centre

BURNS, D. (1980) Feeling Good: The New Mood Therapy New York: Avon Books

CARE QUALITY COMMISSION (2011) Dignity And Nutrition Inspection Programme: National Overview Available at http://www.cqc.org.uk/reviewsandstudies/inspectionprogramme-dignityandnutritionforolderpeople.cfm

CARSON, J.W. et al (2004) Mindfulness Based Relationship Enhancement Behavior Therapy 35, 471-494

CH'EN, K. (1964) Buddhism in China Princeton: Princeton University Press

CHÖDRÖN, P. (1994) Start Where You Are Hammersmith: HarperCollins

CIALDINI, R. (2001) Harnessing the Power of Persuasion Harvard Business Review October

COMMISSION ON DIGNITY IN CARE FOR OLDER PEOPLE (2012) Delivering Dignity available at http://www.nhsconfed.org/priorities/Quality/Partnership-on-dignity/Pages/Draftreportrecommendations.aspx

CRANE, R. (2009) Mindfulness Based Cognitive Therapy Hove:Routledge

CRESWELL, J., IRWIN, M., BURKLUND, S., LIEBERMAN, M., AREVALO, J., MAB, J., BREEN, E. AND COLE, S. (2012) Mindfulness-Based Stress Reduction training reduces loneliness and pro-inflammatory gene expression in older adults: A small randomized controlled trial Brain. Behavior, and Immunity 26 1095-1101

CSIKSZENTMIHALYI, M. (1990) Flow: The Psychology of Optimal Experience. New York: Harper and Row.

CUDDY, A., NORTON, M. and FISKE, S. [2005] This Old Stereotype: The Pervasiveness and Persistence of the Elderly Stereotype Journal of Social Issues, Vol. 61, No. 2, pp. 267-285

CULLEN, M. (2011) Mindfulness-Based Interventions: An Emerging Phenomenon Minfulness 2:186-193

DALAI LAMA and CUTLER, H.C. (1999) The Art of Happiness London: Hodder and Stoughton

DARWIN, J. et al (1979) Against Ageism Newcastle-upon-Tyne: Search Project

DARWIN, J. (2004) Preventing Premature Agreement Reason in Practice: The Journal of Philosophy of Management Volume 4 Number 1

DAVIDSON R.J, KABAT-ZINN J, SCHUMACHER J et al. (2003). Alterations in brain and immune function produced by mindfulness meditation. Psychosomatic Medicine 65 564-570.

De HENNEZEL, M. (2011) The Warmth of the Heart Prevents your Body from Rusting London: Rodale

DEPARTMENT OF HEALTH EXPERT GROUP (2000) Organisation with a Memory The Stationery Office, at http://www.dh.gov.uk/prod_consum_dh/groups/dh_digitalassets/@dh/@en/documents/digitalasset/dh_4065086.pdf

DEPARTMENT OF HEALTH (2010, 2011) Healthy Lives, Healthy People Available at http://www.dh.gov.uk/publications

DEPARTMENT OF HEALTH (2012) Compassion in Practice: Nursing, Midwifery and Care Staff - Our Vision and Strategy

EKMAN, P. (2008) Emotional Awareness, A conversation between the Dalai Lama and Paul Ekman New York: Times Books

EMMONS, R. (2007) Thanks Houghton: Mifflin Harcourt

EMMONS, R. and STERN, R. (2013) Gratitude as a Psychotherapeutic Intervention Journal of Clinical Psychology: In Session. Vol. 69(8). 846-855

EVES, H. (1988) Return to Mathematical Circles, Boston: Prindle, Weber and Schmidt

FLANAGAN, O. (2011) The Bodhisattva's Brain: Buddhism Naturalized Cambridge: The MIT Press

FOWLER, J. and CHRISTAKIS, N. (2008) Dynamic spread of happiness in a large social network: longitudinal analysis over 20 years in the Framingham Heart Study British Medical Journal Vol 338 Page 23

FRANCIS, R. (2013) Report of the Mid Staffordshire NHS Foundation Trust Public Inquiry Executive Summary Available at http://www.midstaffspublicinquiry.com/sites/default/files/report/Executive%20summary.pdf

FRANKL, V.E. (2004) Man's Search for Meaning London: Hodder and Stoughton [first published 1946]

FREDRICKSON, B.L., COHN, M.A., COFFEY, K.A., PEK, J. and FINKEL, S.(2008) Open Hearts Build Lives: Positive Emotions, Induced Through Loving-Kindness Meditation, Build Consequential Personal Resources, Journal of Personality and Social Psychology, Vol. 95, No. 5, 1045-1062

FREDRICKSON, B.L. & LOSADA, M. (2005). Positive affect and the complex dynamics of human flourishing. American Psychologist, 60(7), 678–686.

FREDRICKSON, B. (2009) Positivity Oxford: Oneworld

FRENCH, J. R. P., & RAVEN, B. (1960). The bases of social power. In D. Cartwright & A. Zander, Group dynamics (pp. 150-167). New York:Harper & Row.

FRONSDAL, G. and PANDITA (2005) A Perfect Balance Tricycle Winter pp. 40-45

GARRETT, S. K. , CALDWELL, B. S. , HARRIS, E. C. and GONZALEZ, M. C.(2009) 'Six dimensions of expertise: a more comprehensive definition of cognitive expertise for team coordination', Theoretical Issues in Ergonomics Science, 10: 2, 93 - 105

GERMER, C.K. (2009) The Mindful Path to Self-Compassion New York: Guilford Press

GILBERT, P. (2010a) The Compasionate Mind London: Constable

GILBERT, P. (2010b) Compassion Focused Therapy Hove: Routledge

GILBERT, P. and CHODEN (2013) Mindful Compassion London:Robinson

GIMIAN, C. (Ed.) (1999) The Essential Chogyam Trungpa Boston:Shambhala

GOLEMAN, D. (1995) Emotional Intelligence New York:Bantam Books

GOODALL, H. (2013) The Story of Music London:Chatto and Windus

GREEN RIVER ZEN (2012) How to Move Forward in the Circle of Life Accessed at http://www.greenriverzen.org/2012-winter-intensive-theme

GROSS, R. (2006) The Wisdom in the Anger in McLEOD, M. (ed.) Mindful Politics Boston:Wisdom Publications

GUNARATANA, H. (1991). Mindfulness in plain English. Boston: Wisdom Publications

HALLIWELL, E. (2010) Mindfulness Report Mental Health Foundation available at http://www.livingmindfully.co.uk/downloads/Mindfulness_Report.pdf

HANH, T.N. (1991) The Miracle of Mindfulness London: Rider

HANH, T.N (1993) The Blooming of a Lotus: Guided Meditation Exercises for Healing and Transformation Boston: Beacon Press

HANH, T.N. and CHEUNG, L. (2011) Mindful Eating, Mindful Life: Savour every moment and every bite London: Hay House

HARARI, Y.N. (2008) Combat Flow: Military, Political, and Ethical Dimensions of Subjective Well-Being in War Review of General Psychology Vol. 12, No. 3, 253-264

HARLOW and CANTOR (1996) 'Still Participating After All These Years: a study of life task participation in later life', Journal of Personality and Social Psychology, 71 (6) pp. 1235-49.

HARNAN, S., COOPER, K., POKU, E. and WOOD, H. (2013) A Research Report of the Therapeutic effects of Yoga for Health and Wellbeing" University of Sheffield report prepared for the British Wheel Of Yoga

HEALTHCARE COMMISSION (2009) Investigation into Mid Staffordshire NHS Foundation Trust Available at http://www.midstaffsinquiry.com/assets/docs/Healthcare%20Commission%20report.pdf

HONEY, P. and MUMFORD, A. (1992) The Manual of Learning Styles Peter Honey Publications

HOUSE OF LORDS (2013) Ready for Ageing Report of Select Committee on Public Service and Demographic Change

HUTCHERSON, C. et al (2008) Loving-Kindness Meditation Increases Social Connectedness Emotion Vol 8 No 5 720-24

JACKSON, N. (undated) Unselfish Joy: A Neglected Virtue (from Metta, The Journal of the Buddhist Federation of Australia, Vol. 12, No. 2.) Accessed at http://www.accesstoinsight.org/lib/authors/various/wheel170.html

JAIN, S., SHAPIRO, S., SWANICK, S., ROESCH, S., MILLS, P., BELL, I., & SCHWARTZ, G. (2007). A randomized controlled trial of mindfulness meditation versus relaxation training: effects on distress, positive states of mind, rumination, and distraction. Annals of Behavioral Medicine, 3:11-21

JALON, A. (2003) Meditating On War And Guilt, Zen Says It's Sorry New York Times: Posted At http://www.nytimes.com/2003/01/11/Books/Meditating-On-War-And-Guilt-Zen-Says-It-S-Sorry.Html

JAMISON, C (2009) Finding Happiness London:Phoenix

JHA, A.P., KROMPINGER, J, BAIME, M.J. (2007). Mindfulness training modifies subsystems of attention. Cognitive, Affective & Behavioral Neuroscience 7 109-119.

JIYU-KENNETT, P. (1990) The Liturgy of the Order of Buddhist Contemplatives for the Laity Mt. Shasta:Shasta Abbey Press

JOHNSON, D., PENN, D., FREDRICKSON, B., MEYER, P., KRING, A. and BRANTLEY, M. (2009) Loving-kindness meditation to enhance recovery from negative symptoms of schizophrenia Journal of Clinical Psychology Volume 65, Issue 5, pages 499–509

JOYCE, J. (1914) Dubliners London: Grant Richards

KABAT-ZINN J., (1990), Full Catastrophe Living: Using the Wisdom of Your Body and Mind to Face Stress, Pain and Illness. Delta

KABAT-ZINN J., (1994), Mindfulness meditation for everyday life. Piatkus:New York

KABAT-ZINN J., (2005), Coming to Our Senses: Healing Ourselves and the World Through Mindfulness. Piatkus: New York

KABAT-ZINN J., (2005b), Wherever you go there you are: Mindfulness meditation in everyday life Hyperion

KITE, M., DEAUX, K. & MILE, M. (1991) Stereotypes of Young and Old: Does Age Outweigh Gender? Psychology and Aging Vol 6 No 1, 19-27

KOLB, D. (1984) Experiential Learning: Experience as the source of learning and development Englewood Cliffs: Prentice-Hall

KONNERT, C., DOBSON, K. & STELMACH, L. (2009) The prevention of depression in nursing home residents: a randomized clinical trial of cognitive-behavioural therapy Aging and Mental Health Vol 13 No 2 pp 288-299

LAIDLAW, K., THOMPSON, L., GALLAGHER-THOMPSON, D. and DICK-SISKIN, L. [2003] Cognitive Behaviour Therapy with Older People Chichester: Wiley

LANGER, E. (1997) Mindfulness: The Power of mindful learning. Reading, MA: Perseus Books.

LANGER, E. (2009) Counterclockwise London:Hodder and Stroughton

LEVINE, M (2009) The Positive Psychology of Buddhism and Yoga London: Routledge

LEVINTHAL, D. and RERUP, C. (2006) Crossing An Apparent Chasm: Bridging Mindful and Less-Mindful Perspectives on Organizational Learning Organization Science Vol 17 No 4 pp 502-513

LEVY, B.R. (2001) Eradication of ageism requires addressing the enemy within The Gerontologist; Oct 2001; 41, 5

LEVY, B.R., SLADE, M., KUNKEL, S. & KASL, S. (2002) Longevity Increased by Positive Self-Perceptions of Aging Journal of Personality and Social Psychology, Vol. 83, No. 2, 261-270

LEVY, B.R. (2003) Mind Matters: Cognitive and Physical Effects of Aging Self-Stereotypes Journal of Gerontology Vol. 58B, No. 4, pp203-211

LINEHAN, M.M. (1993) Cognitive-Behavioral Treatment of Borderline Personality Disorder New York: Guilford Press

LOCAL GOVERNMENT IMPROVEMENT AND DEVELOPMENT AND THE NATIONAL MENTAL HEALTH DEVELOPMENT UNIT (2010) The Role Of Local Government In Promoting Wellbeing Available at http://www.local.gov.uk/c/ document_library/get_file?uuid=867e0406-35a5-4e91-910d-6b13305d2319&groupId=10171

LOW, A. (2006) Hakuin on Kensho: The Four Ways of Knowing London:Shambhala

LOY, D. (1995) Is Zen Buddhism? The Eastern Buddhist Vol. 28, No. 2 (Autumn) pp. 273-286

LOY, D. (2006) Wego: the Social Roots of Suffering in McLeod, M. (Ed.) Mindful Politics Somerville:Wisdom Publications

LUKES, S. (2005) Power: A Radical View Basingstoke:Palgrave-Macmillan

LUTZ, A., DAVIDSON, R. et al (2008) Regulation of the Neural Circuitry of Emotion by Compassion Meditation: Effects of Meditative Expertise PLoS ONE 3(3): e1897. doi:10.1371/journal.pone.0001897

LYNCH T. & BRONNER L. (2006). Mindfulness and dialectical behaviour therapy (DBT): application with depressed older adults with personality disorders. In: BAER RA (ed). Mindfulness-based treatment approaches: clinician's guide to evidence base and applications. San Diego: Academic Press (pp217-233).

LYUBOMIRSKY, S. (2007) The How of Happiness London: Piatkus

MACASKILL. A (2002). Heal the hurt: How to forgive and move on. London; Sheldon Press.

MACKENZIE, C., POULIN, P. and SEIDMAN-CARLSON, R. (2006) A Brief Mindfulness-based Reduction Intervention for Nurses and Nurse Aides Applied Nursing Research 19, 105-109

MARMOT, M. (2010) Fair Society, Healthy Lives Available at http://Www.Instituteofhealthequity.Org/Projects/Fair-Society-Healthy-Lives-The-Marmot-Review

MCBEE, L.(2003) Mindfulness practice with the frail elderly and their caregivers Topics in Geriatric Rehabilitation Vol 19 No 4 pp 257-264

MCBEE, L. (2009) Mindfulness-based Elder Care:Communicating Mindfulness to Frail Elders and their Caregivers, in Didonna, F. (2009) Clinical Handbook of Mindfulness Springer Science-Business Media

MCCOWN, D. and REIBEL, D (2009) Mindfulness and Mindfulness-Based Stress Reduction Integrative Psychiatry, Weil Integrative Medicine Library, Edited by B. Beitman and D. Monti, Oxford University Press

MCCOWN, D., REIBEL, D. and MICOZZI, M. (2010) Teaching Mindfulness New York:Springer

MCGILL, I. and BEATY, L. (2001) Action Learning London:Kogan Page

MCCULLOUGH, M.E. (2002) Savoring Life, Past and Present: Explaining What Hope and Gratitude Share in Common Psychological Inquiry, Vol. 13, No. 4 (2002), pp. 302-304

MCLEOD, K. (2001) Wake Up To Your Life New York: HarperCollins

McWILLIAMS, S. (1996) A Contemplative Model for Higher Education Paper presented at the conference "Teaching From Within," Blue Sky Associates, Northfield, Minnesota Accessed at http://public.csusm.edu/mcwilliams/My%20Publications/Contemplative%20Higher%20Ed.pdf

MEDICAL NEWS TODAY (2010) Transcendental Meditation Shown To Reduce Depression: New Studies 8 April. Accessed at http://www.medicalnewstoday.com/articles/184805.php

MENAHEM, S. and LOVE, M. (2013) Forgiveness in Psychotherapy: The Key to Healing Journal of Clinical Psychology: In Session. Vol. 69(8). 829-835

MENTAL HEALTH FOUNDATION (2010) Mindfulness Report

MINGYUR, Y. RINPOCHE (2007) The Joy of Living London:Transworld Publishers

MORGAN, G. (1988) Riding the Waves of Change San Francisco:Jossey-Bass

MORONE, N. & GRECO, C. (2007) Mind-body interventions for chronic pain in older adults: a structured review Pain Medicine Vol 8 No 4 pp 359-375

MORONE, N. , GRECO, C. & WEINER, D. (2008) Mindfulness meditation for the treatement of chronic low back pain in older adults: A randomized controlled pilot study Pain Vol 134 Issue 3 pp 310-319

MOULTON, C., REGEHR, G., MYLOPOULOS, M. and MACRAE, H. (2007) Slowing down when you should: A new model of expert judgment Academic Medicine Vol 82 No 10

MUSCOLINO, J. & CIPRIANI, S. (2004) Pilates and the "powerhouse" I Journal of Bodywork and Movement Therapies 8, 15-24

NAIRN, R. (1999) Diamond Mind Boston:Shambhala

BHIKKHU NANAMOLI and BHIKKHU BODHI (translators) (2005) The Middle Length Discourses of the Buddha: A Translation of the Majjhima Nikaya Boston: Wisdom

NARAYANASAMY, A (2010) Recognising spiritual needs in McSherry, W. and Ross, L. (Eds.) Spiritual Assessment in Healthcare Practice Keswick:M&K Update Ltd

NEFF, K. (2011) Self-Compassion London:Hodder & Stoughton

NAROPA Online Faculty Panel (2005) Best Practices In Online Contemplative Education Accessed at

http://www.naropa.edu/documents/departments/extended-studies/distance-learning/best-practices-in-online-contemplative-ed.pdf

NETO, F. (2007) Forgiveness, personality and gratitude Personality and Individual Differences 43:2313-2323

NEW ECONOMICS FOUNDATION (2008) Five Ways to Wellbeing Available at http://dnwssx4l7gl7s.cloudfront.net/nefoundation/default/page/-/files/Five_Ways_to_Wellbeing.pdf

NONAKA, I. and TAKEUCHI, H. (1995) The Knowledge-Creating Company New York:Oxford University Press

NORBU, T. (2012) Magic Dance: The Display of the Self-nature of the Five Wisdom Dākinīs Boston:Shambhala

NYANAPONIKA THERA (1994) The Four Sublime States Buddha Dharma Education Association downloaded from http://www.accesstoinsight.org/lib/authors/nyanaponika/wheel006.html

NYANAPONIKA THERA (1998) (Translator) Sallatha Sutta: The Dart, published by the Buddhist Publication Society and available at http://www.vipassana.com/canon/samyutta/sn36-6b.php

NYANAPONIKA THERA, JACKSON, N., KNIGHT, C. and OATES, L. (2005) Mudita: The Buddha's Teaching on Unselfish Joy downloaded from http://www.accesstoinsight.org/lib/authors/various/wheel170.html

NYAPONIKA THERA and BHIKKHU BODHI (2007) Numerical Discourses of the Buddha: An Anthology of Suttas from the Anguttara Nikaya Kandy: Buddhist Publication Society

NYANASATTA THERA (1994) Satipatthana Sutta: The Foundations of Mindfulness, translated from the Pali Available at http://www.accesstoinsight.org/tipitaka/mn/mn.010.nysa.html

NYE, J. (2004) Soft Power and American Foreign Policy Political Science Quarterly Volume 119 Number 2 2004 pp 255-270

O'BRIEN COUSINS, S. (2000) "My Heart Couldn't Take It": Older Women's Beliefs About Exercise Benefits and Risks Journal of Gerontology, Vol. 55B, No. 5, P283 P294

OKUN, M et al (1984) 'The Social Activity/Subjective Well-Being Relation: a quantitative synthesis' Research on Aging, 6 (1) pp. 45-65.

OMAN, D. , SHAPIRO, S., THORESEN, C., PLANTE, T. and FLINDERS, T. (2008) Meditation lowers stress and supports forgiveness among college students; a randomized controlled trial Journal of American College Health Vol 56 no 5 pp 569-578

ORTNER, D., KILNER, S. and ZELAZO, P. (2007) Mindfulness meditation and reduced emotional interference on a cognitive task Motivation and Emotion Volume 31, Number 4, 271-283,

OTAKE, K. et al (2006) Happy people become happier through kindness: A counting kindnesses intervention Journal of Happiness Studies 7:361:375

POLANYI, M. (1958) Personal Knowledge: Towards a Post-Critical Philosophy. University of Chicago Press

RAVEN, B. H. (1992) A power/interaction model of interpersonal influence: French and Raven thirty years later Journal of Social Behavior & Personality, Vol 7(2), 217-244.

REJESKI, W.J. (2008) Mindfulness: Reconnecting the Body and Mind in Geriatric Medicine and Gerontology The Gerontologist April 2008, 48, 2

REVANS, R. (1982) The Immemorial Precursor: Action Learning Past and Present in The Origins and Growth of Action Learning pp 529-545 Lund: Studentlitteratur

RICARD, M. (2007) Happiness: A Guide to Developing Life's Most Important Skill London: Atlantic Books

RICHMOND, L. (1999) Work as a Spiritual Practice London: Judy Piatkus

RICHMOND, L (2004) A Whole Life's Work New York: Atria Books

RICHMOND, L (2012) Aging as a Spiritual Practice, New York: Gotham

ROCKWELL, I. (2002) The Five Wisdom Energies Boston:Shambhala

ROCKWELL, I. (2003) The Five Wisdoms: A Contemplative Approach to Integrative Learning Accessed at http://www.fivewisdomsinstitute.com/wp-content/uploads/resources/articles_interviews/Integrative_Learning.pdf

ROGERS, C. (1969) Freedom to Learn Columbus, Ohio:Merrill

ROSENZWEIG, S., REIBEL, D., GREESON, J., BRAINARD, G., & HOJAT, M. (2003). Mindfulness-based stress reduction lowers psychological distress in medical students. Teaching and Learning in Medicine, 15(2):88-92.

ROSENZWEIG, D. (2013) The Sisters of Mindfulness Journal of Clinical Psychology: In Session. Vol. 69(8). 793-804

ROTH, B. & CALLE-MESA, L. (2006). Mindfulness-based stress reduction with Spanish- and English-speaking inner-city medical patients. In R.A. Baer (Ed.). (2006). Mindfulness-based treatment approaches: Clinician's guide to evidence base and applications. Boston: Elsevier Academic Press.

SALZBERG, S. (1995) Loving Kindness Boston: Shambhala

SANGHARAKSHITA (1957, Seventh edition 1993) A Survey of Buddhism Glasgow:Windhorse

SANTORELLI S., (1999), Heal Thyself: Lessons on Mindfulness in Medicine, Bell. Tower.

SCHNEIDER, S. (2001) In Search of Realistic Optimism American Psychologist March 250-262

SEGAL Z.V., WILLIAMS J.M.G. & TEASDALE J.D., (First Edition:2002; second edition:2013), Mindfulness based Cognitive Therapy for Depression. A New Approach to Preventing Relapse. New York: Guilford Press.

SELIGMAN, M.E.P. and CSIKSZENTMIHALYI, M. (2000) Positive Psychology American Psychologist

SELIGMAN, M.E.P. (2003) Authentic Happiness London: Nicholas Brealey

SELIGMAN, M.E.P. (2006) Learned Optimism New York: Vintage Books

SELIGMAN, M.E.P. (2011) Flourishing London: Nicholas Brealey

SHAPIRO, S.L. and SCHWARTZ, G.E. (2000). The role of intention in self-regulation: Toward intentional systemic mindfulness. In M. BOEKAERTS, P.R. PINTRICH, & M. ZEIDNER (Eds.), Handbook of self-regulation (pp. 253 273). San Diego, CA: Academic Press.

SHAPIRO, S. L., CARLSON, L., ASTIN, J., & FREEDMAN, B. (2006) Mechanisms of mindfulness Journal of Clinical Psychology, 1 14

SHAPIRO, A., WARREN BROWN, K. AND BIEGEL, G. (2007) Teaching Self-Care to Caregivers: Effects of Mindfulness-Based Stress Reduction on the Mental Health of Therapists in Training Training and Education in Professional Psychology, Vol. 1, No. 2, 105-115

SHAPIRO, S., BROWN, K. and ASTIN, J, (2008) Toward the Integration of Meditation into Higher Education: A Review of Research Prepared for the Center for Contemplative Mind in Society, available at http://www.contemplativemind.org/programs/academic/MedandHigherEd.pdf

SHAPIRO, S.L., & IZETT, C. (2008). Meditation: A universal tool for cultivating empathy. In D.Hick, & T.Bien (Eds), Mindfulness and the therapeutic relationship (pp. 161–175). New York: Guilford Press.

SMITH, A (2006). "Like waking up from a dream": mindfulness training for older people with anxiety and depression. In: Baer RA (ed) Mindfulness-based treatment approaches: clinician's guide to evidence base and applications San Diego: Academic Press (pp191-212).

SMITH, A. , GRAHAM, L. and SENTHINATHAN, S.(2007) 'Mindfulness-based cognitive therapy for recurring depression in older people: A qualitative study', Aging & Mental Health, 11: 3, 346-357

SŌTŌSHU SHUMUCHO The Recall of "The History of Sōtō Zen Overseas Missionary Activities" in Zen Quarterly Vol 9 No 4 (1998), and Vol. 10. No. 1 (1999) Sotoshu Shumucho Tokyo

SPLEVINS, K., SMITH, A. & SIMPSON, J. (2009) Do Improvements in emotional distress correlate with becoming more mindful? A study of older adults. Aging & Mental Health Vol 13 No 3 pp328-335

STACEY, M. (1995) Advanced Driver's Handbook London: Kogan Page

STONE, H. and STONE, S. (1989a) Embracing Our Selves: The Voice Dialogue Manual Novato:Naturaj

STONE, H. and STONE, S. (1989b) Embracing Each Other Albion:Delos

SUBER, P. (1996) Classical Skepticism: Issues and Problems at http://www.earlham.edu/~peters/writing/skept.htm

SUZUKI, S. (1970) Zen Mind, Beginner's Mind. New York: Weatherhill

SWEARER, D.K. (1997) The Worldliness of Buddhism The Wilson Quarterly Vol 21 No 2 Positive Psychology 81-93

TAN, C-M (2012) Search Inside Yourself London:Harper-Collins

TEASDALE, J. D., SEGAL, Z. V., WILLIAMS, J. M. G., RIDGEWAY, V. A., SOULSBY, J. M., & LAU, M. A. (2000). Prevention of relapse/recurrence in major depression by mindfulness-based cognitive therapy Journal of Consulting and Clinical Psychology, 68, 615–623.

THRANGU RINPOCHE, K. (1998) The Five Buddha Families and the Eight Consciousnesses Boulder:Namo

THRANGU RINPOCHE, K. (2002) Everyday Consciousness and Primordial Awareness Ithaca:Snow Lion

TURNER, K. (2010) The Promotion of Successful Aging through Mindfulness Skills Training Doctorate in Social Work Dissertations. Available at http://repository.upenn.edu/edissertations_sp2/1

VAILLANT, G. (1993) The Wisdom of the Ego Cambridge:Harvard University Press

VARELA, F and SHEAR, J (1999) First-Person Methodologies: What, Why, How? In Journal of Consciousness Studies Vol 6, No 2-3, Positive Psychology 1-14.

VARELA, F. J., THOMPSON, E. and ROSCH, E. (1993) The Embodied Mind MIT Press

VICTORIA, B.D. (c2000) Engaged Buddhism: A Skeleton in the Closet? Research article published at http://www.globalbuddhism.org/2/victoria011.html

VICTORIA, B.D. (2006) Zen at War , 2nd Edition, Oxford: Rowman and Littlefield

WALLACE, B.A. (2004) The Four Immeasurables Ithaca: Snow Lion

WALLACE, B.A. (2006) The Attention Revolution Somerville:Wisdom

WALLACE, B.A. (2008) A Mindful Balance Tricycle Spring 2008, available at http://www.tricycle.com/a-mindful-balance?page=0,1

WALSH, R. (2011) Lifestyle and Mental Health American Psychologist October, 579-592

WALSHE, M (translator) (1995) The Long Discourses of the Buddha: A Translation of the Digha Nikaya Boston: Wisdom Publications

WALSHE, M (translator) (2010) Samyutta Nikara: An Anthology Buddhist Publication Society Downloaded from http://www.accesstoinsight.org/lib/authors/walshe/wheel318.html

WEICK, K.E. and SUTCLIFFE, K.M. (2007) Managing the Unexpected John Wiley and Sons

WHITE PLUM ASANGA (2011) Statement of the Board: available at http://www.whiteplum.org/announcements.html

WHYTE, D. (2002) The Heart Aroused: Poetry and the Preservation of the Soul in Corporate America New York:Doubleday

WILLIAMS, M. and PENMAN, D. (2011) Mindfulness: a practical guide to finding peace in a frantic world London:Piatkus

WORLD HEALTH ORGANIZATION (2011) Global Health and Aging Available from WHO at http://www.who.int/ageing/publications/global_health/en/

YOUNG, L. AND BAIME, M. (2010) Mindfulness-Based Stress Reduction: Effect on Emotional Distress in Older Adults Complementary Health Practice Review 15: 59

ZEN CENTER OF LOS ANGELES (2012) The ZCLA Curriculum accessed at http://www.zencenter.com/Programs/Curriculum/documents/ TheZCLACurriculumfinalwordversionJuly132012.pdf

ZIMBARDO, P. (2007) The Lucifer Effect: How Good People Turn Evil Reading:Rider